A FRAGILE BEAUTY

A FRAGILE BEAUTY

—

JOHN NICHOLS' MILAGRO COUNTRY

—

TEXT AND PHOTOGRAPHS FROM HIS LIFE AND WORK

�܀P

GIBBS M. SMITH, INC.
PEREGRINE SMITH BOOKS
SALT LAKE CITY

First edition

91 90 89 88 87   5 4 3 2 1

Copyright © 1987 by John Treadwell Nichols.
Published by Gibbs M. Smith, Inc., P.O. Box 667,
Layton, UT 84041

Design by J. Scott Knudsen

Manufactured in Japan

Library of Congress Cataloging-in-Publication Data

Nichols, John Treadwell, 1940 –
  A fragile beauty : John Nichols' Milagro country:
text and photographs from his life and
work / foreword by Robert Redford.
    p.   cm.
  ISBN 0-87905-282-1 : $34.95
  1. Nichols, John Treadwell, 1940 –
– Homes and haunts – New Mexico – Taos Region.
2. Nichols, John Treadwell, 1940 – Milagro beanfield
war. 3. Taos Region (N.M.) – Description and travel.
4. Taos Region (N.M.) – Social life and customs.
5. Novelists, American – 20th century
– Biography.   I. Title.
PS3564.I274Z464 1987
818'.5403 – dc19
[B]

For JUANITA

With so much love and gratitude for the

Sheep Trailer, the Monet Garden, all

the days of sharing our magic journey

together . . . and a thousand

evenings on the mesa.

"Joy belongs to the relentless!"

FOREWORD

John Nichols' Milagro Country—the mountainous region of northern New Mexico—is a contradiction.

It is many-layered and demands much of those who find themselves in its presence. It escapes definition. It is gentle yet raw, graceful, unpredictable, cruel and fragile and full of an ancient peace.

Here one feels embraced by the traditions and customs of the land, yet somehow kept from them. Its unyielding secrecy has eluded many and the quest to understand it has driven some mad. It has been dug, photographed, filmed, damned, shot at, plowed and still its mystery continues. It is a puzzled scratch on the head of America's western frontier. It holds the promise of some vague fulfillment, like the new life sought by one battered by the holocaust of big-city living. So many come to have it, to embrace its magic, to steep in it, only to move away within a short time, frustrated.

These mountains and their attendant valleys belong to the spirits of the dead and the cultures that have followed in their footsteps. They belong to the tourist only in passing and in pictures. They are best survived by the natives who settled here—themselves a mix of Indian, Mexican and Spanish, then the Anglo American and God knows what else thrown in.

John Nichols understands this, himself much like the land he treasures and stays pledged to keep. Kind, angry, gentle, robust and wise, he rolls easily about this land, loving it, knowing it, wearing a grin. It is a real smile, though, like the land, winking at all that is silly and comic, all that which is supposed to work, but doesn't, and especially that which in its natural state is beautiful.

His may be a windmill fight. But it is a noble one, and I salute it.

Robert Redford
New York, May 1987

ACKNOWLEDGMENTS

Portions of the introductory essay to this book were originally published in *American Film Magazine,* May 1987.

Grateful acknowledgment is made to Alfred A. Knopf for permission to reprint from *If Mountains Die* (photographs by William Davis, text by John Nichols), copyright © 1979 by John Nichols and William Davis. Used by permission. Passages excerpted from this work appear on pages 29-41, 115-120, 129-134.

Grateful acknowledgment is made to Henry Holt and Company, Inc. for permission to reprint from:

The Last Beautiful Days of Autumn by John Nichols, copyright © 1982 by John Tread-well Nichols. Passages excerpted from this work appear on pages 45-54, 81-110, 139-146.

The Milagro Beanfield War by John Nichols, copyright © 1974 by John Nichols. Passages excerpted from this work appear on pages 120-124.

Grateful acknowledgment is made to Gibbs M. Smith, Inc. for permission to reprint from *On the Mesa,* copyright © 1986 by Gibbs M. Smith, Inc. in the name of the author, John Treadwell Nichols. Passages excerpted from this work appear on pages 55-76, 124-129.

Demonstrators at Taos County Courthouse protesting the police shooting of a
Chicano youth. Cover photo, **New Mexico Review,** *September 1971.*

INTRODUCTION

—

From the Chiricahua

—

Mountains to

—

Hollywood and Vine

—

The Milagro Beanfield War was the first book I published while living in New Mexico. As such, it broke ground for my other novels like *The Magic Journey* and *The Nirvana Blues,* and for the non-fiction books: *If Mountains Die* (with photographs by William Davis), *The Last Beautiful Days of Autumn,* and *On the Mesa.* Different as the emphasis of each of these books may be, they all deal with questions of land, cultural ethics, problems of ecology, economics, history, and human survival.

In the summer and autumn of 1986, *Milagro* was made into a film produced by Moctesuma Esparza and Robert Redford, and directed by Redford. I write this in January 1987, months before I will see even a rough cut of the film. So how it turned out is still up for grabs. But to coincide with the release of the film, Gibbs Smith suggested I do a book of photographs about

the "Milagro country" of northern New Mexico. In it would be included excerpts from four of the six works I just mentioned: *Milagro* and the three non-fiction books. They all have material related to the themes of *Milagro*—specifically land, land-based culture, and the struggle to both defend and exault that balanced way of life. In this sense, both the film and this book speak for, and are a summation of, my seventeen years of life and work in New Mexico.

My hopes for this book are the same hopes I had when I encouraged the *Milagro* movie to be made. Specifically, I wanted the Redford–Esparza production to echo the politics, the social concerns, and the historical and ecological perspectives of my work. If the film succeeds in that, then the convoluted process of nursing it through the Hollywood maze will have been worth it.

John Muir once said, "Whenever we try

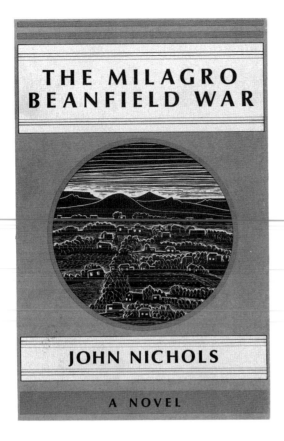

to pick out anything by itself, we find it connected to everything else in the universe." I have always kept that in mind while writing about the land, people, heartaches of northern New Mexico. To extoll the fragile beauty of the Taos Valley in words, photographs, or in a film, is to sing the praises of, and to demand consideration for, the entire earth.

The implications are always universal.

I t's an old adage that the origins of things reveal their meanings. My love of the Southwest began in the summer of 1957, when I first visited New Mexico and Arizona. I was sixteen. I spent a week in Taos plastering a friend's adobe house, then headed down to a New York Museum of Natural History research station in Portal, Arizona, not far from the Mexican border. There I spent some time as a ranchhand, as a carpenter, and I helped scientists collect bugs, beetles, butterflies. I also fought a few

forest fires as a volunteer smoke chaser, earning $1.50 around the clock.

It was a dream summer in a dream territory. At dusk I cruised along desert highways, hunting rattlers and gopher snakes. I collected tiger beetles, grasshoppers (with tiny mites behind their gills), and lizards to be used in various experiments. The forest fires occurred in the Chiricahua Mountains. Most of the men I worked with were either Chicanos from Rodeo, New Mexico, or Mexican nationals, illegally in the country, allowed to stay so long as the government needed them.

We hiked into the hills on foot; one time we traveled in on horseback. Dozens of scorpions scurried ahead of us as we chopped our fire lines. Small airplanes dropped radios and supplies at our targets of colorful parachute silk. The language was Spanish, and I wanted desperately to learn it; naturally, I picked up every swearword in the book. Large mule deer herds scampered across high country meadows; fields of rich, flowering penstemon were inundated by hummingbirds.

On several weekends I traveled with my new friends by pickup truck to Agua Prieta, Mexico. One-armed Pedro held the wheel; the rest of us lay drunk and singing in the bed. We staggered through the red light district, raucously hooting mariachi tunes. I sat nervously on bar stools while chipper prostitutes teased me for not joining my cheerful compatriots in the back rooms. Instead, I bought switchblade knives and smuggled them back across the border.

At summer's end I hailed a bus during a flash flood in Lordsburg, New Mexico. Already a "novel" about the Southwest was percolating in my mind. During my senior year at prep school, I wrote the story which might be called a distant preview of *The Milagro Beanfield War.* Only forty pages long, entitled "The Journey," it was about a Chicano—a mestizo kid—named Francisco Morelos, who led his blind, Indian grandfather up into the mountains to die.

Much of the story incorporated landscape, weather, an atmosphere close to the earth, an evident love of wild country:

The climbing became steeper and more than once the horses slipped on the wet stones in the trail. Then they rounded a curve in the trail and came into a clearing on the side of the mountain. Just as they entered the clearing, the sun burst into view and Francisco exclaimed at the rainbow, which arced over the flats below. The air was clear and he could see far out on the desert. He could see the pueblos, and the town beyond. His Tata listened as Francisco described the rainbow, and the tiny specks which were the buffalo herd, and the thin curls of smoke coming from the pueblos. Francisco described to him the fields, and the little circular fingerprints on the land made by the plows. The desert country was resting in all the bright colors of autumn and there was a patchwork of the mellow desert browns and reds in the places where the trees were. When Francisco looked at the old man he saw that he was smiling.

I do not recall a great passion for returning to the Southwest, back then: life was too busy on other fronts. Yet occasionally I made forays into the outskirts of Spanish-speaking culture. For a while, after reading Tom Lea's book, *The Wonderful Country,* that was my favorite novel. At Hamilton College, my writing often emulated Hemingway. Many of my early stories were sprinkled with Spanish words. In the school literary magazine I published a long story about whores, cripples, gangsters, and Gaudí in Barcelona. I dreamed about Pamplona, bullfighting, gun-running to Cuba. In college I also wrote a novel about racism in the South called *Don't Be Forlorn.* My most emphatic personal experience with overt racism occurred when I walked into a Troy, New York, bar and jokingly ordered a beer in Spanish. The man next to me snarled, "You fucking spick!" and punched me in the mouth. I went down, poleaxed, and the bar

erupted into a free-for-all.

Though my mother was French, she had been raised in Barcelona. While still a teenager, in 1932, she traveled to the southwestern United States and spent much time visiting the pueblos near Santa Fe. When I was two, she died . . . and I never made it to Europe until summertime 1960, when a friend and I visited my grandmother in Barcelona. We attended a bullfighting school run by an aged matador, Pedrucho. Then we traveled around Spain, following the corridas. We immersed ourselves in Joselito, Belmonte, Manolete, Arruza, and then current matadors like Dominguín, Ordoñez, Paco Camino, and a fledgling madman, still fighting novilladas, El Cordobés. At the end of August we departed a Pan American flight in New York wearing rejoneador costumes and knee-high botas; magenta and yellow bullfighting capes were draped over our shoulders. We must have resembled cartoon idiots, but we *felt* like macho Iberian studs.

My mother, Monique Robert, out West, 1933.

3

Posing with the Sanchez brothers in bullfighting school, Barcelona, 1960. Photograph by Bill Willis.

The author executes a clumsy veronica. Photograph by Bill Willis.

After college, I returned to Spain for a year and finally taught myself French and Spanish. Writers who helped and influenced me were Juan Ramón Jiménez, García Lorca, Pablo Neruda, Miguel Ángel Asturias. When I moved to New York in 1963, I settled in a largely Italian and Puerto Rican neighborhood, a coherent and together community. For two years I hung out with a pandilla of Latin Americans from Argentina and Chile. Among them was a 300-pound, red-haired behemouth named Aureo Roldán, who ran an empanada stand; also a shy boxer, Oscar Bonavena, who was being groomed for a shot at the heavyweight title. Years later, Bonavena was shot to death outside a Nevada brothel; Roldán disappeared in a camper truck on his way to sell empanadas in Alaska.

While all together, however, we had some rare times: drunken brawls at McSorley's Old Ale House; wild poetry and corrido-spouting dinners in Chinatown; endless arguments about Firpo, Carlos Gardel, Juan Perón, Juan Fangio . . . Evita. I wrote a novel about that gang called *The Empanada*

Brotherhood. It was never published. But I think the energy of that small book was *Milagro* all the way.

In 1964 I took a bus from New York to Guatemala City to visit a friend. What began

Age 23, down in Chichicastenango, Guatemala. Photograph by F. M. Weld.

as a lark wound up radically changing my life. Though truly colorful, Guatemala was — still is, of course — a frightfully tormented country. I'd never experienced such poverty, such a devastated culture. I was shocked to realize how deeply my own country bore responsibility for the miserable conditions in Central America.

Back in New York, the reverberations of Guatemala led me to protest the ever-widening Vietnam War. I yearned to merge a social conscience with my fledgling art. During the rest of the sixties, I helped organize against the war for groups like SANE, the Moratorium, MDS. I attended study groups, many demonstrations — marched on the Pentagon in 1967. Along the way my political and economic philosophies were completely altered. Karl Marx made more sense than Adam Smith. The novels I wrote tried to incorporate left polemics. They dealt with United States imperialism, the moral bankruptcy of the Vietnam War,

U.S. history viewed as systematic genocide against Native Americans, terracide against the planet.

The books were angry (and unsuccessful) diatribes against our economic culture of planned obsolescence and conspicuous consumption. They came from a writer increasingly disenchanted by the inequalities of American life. I read voraciously: *The Autobiography of Malcolm X, A History of Standard Oil, The Tragedy of American Diplomacy* — Marx, Engels, Lenin, Thorsten Veblen, Matthew Josephson, Charles and Mary Beard.

When, in 1969, I left New York, New Mexico was a logical place to head for. Not because of land or majestic weather. Rather, New Mexico seemed to resemble a colonial country where political struggle could be as clearly focused as it was in four-fifths of the rest of the world. I had been reading a newspaper called *El Grito Del Norte,* published by Betita Martínez in Española,

5

Reies Tijerina, whose land grant movement brought a new political awareness to New Mexico.

Gorge; I was even captivated by the cruel, alarming iciness of winter weather at 7,000 feet, in the shadow of 13,000-foot mountains.

The land was essential to the rhythm of life in Taos, and all of it was threatened by one form of development or another. Sadly, I quickly came to realize, the longtime caretakers of the valley were being driven out.

Shortly after reaching Taos, I began writing for a muckraking journal called *The New Mexico Review.* Originally founded by a fellow named Ed Schwartz, who considered the paper a legislative watchdog, it was soon taken over by a Princeton hockey player and fledgling lawyer named Em Hall, and his buddy, Jim Bensfield. They couldn't pay salaries. Indeed, I doubt they ever even paid for a story. To make up for this shortcoming—at least in my case—Em Hall played center on a line with me in an Albuquerque ice hockey league, and he continuously fed me the puck so that I could score goals. Such unselfishness from Em, given his own savage lust to rack up points, touched me more than I would have been moved if he'd simply paid me for my writing, but had then refused to pass the puck!

The *Review* ran on a shoestring and a prayer, a bit of advertising revenue, and small grants and donations from the lunatic political fringe. Hall and Bensfield would have liked it to be a southwestern *New Yorker,* with a bit of aristocratic trout fishing thrown in. Unfortunately, just to keep the paper going, they were forced to let a collective run it. And much of the collective—including yours truly—had more radical dreams for the rag. Of course, the farther left we went, the harder it was to dislodge bread, even from the liberals. And by 1972 the *Review* was going down fast. Bensfield and Hall turned over the editing to Jim Rowen, George McGovern's son-in-law. But Rowen grew disillusioned after a few issues and decided to bag the venture. I couldn't bear

near Santa Fe. Copies showed up regularly at the 8th Street Bookstore in Manhattan. I also read Stan Steiner's books about the Indian and Chicano movements, *The New Indians* and *La Raza.* I was fascinated by Reies Tijerina's land grant politics which had culminated in an armed raid on the Tierra Amarilla, New Mexico, courthouse in 1967.

Yet in the end, in New Mexico, it was the land, as much as the social and economic situation, which fired up my energy and gifted a new life I had not dreamed of. I hiked the wide sagebrush mesa west of Taos, gathered piñon wood in hills made redolent by autumn wildflowers, worked on the irrigation ditches that carried water to gardens I began to grow. And I soon grew to love fishing in the prehistoric Rio Grande

to watch it die, because I loved it, and also, I suppose, because the *Review* was the only organ to publish me since 1966!

So I became volunteer editor for the last three issues in 1972. A Taos artist, Rini Templeton—who would later illustrate *The Milagro Beanfield War*—taught me about makeup, layout, theories of design; together we kept the magazine going.

But by November I was photographing, writing, and cartooning almost the entire issue. And, exhausted, dismayed, I gave up; the *Review* finally expired, never to be resurrected again, except as *The Voice of the People* in *Milagro*.

For those three years the magazine provided a forum for my views. It also gave me an excuse to research the valley in which I lived. My first article concerned a friend, Joe Cisneros, who had been fired by a molybdenum mine in Questa, a town half an hour north of Taos. My style, at that time, was not exactly laid back and "objective":

> *In short, Joe Cisneros has committed the unpardonable sin of confronting Corporate America. Almost single-handedly he has locked himself in combat with the monolith . . . Joe was fired for trying to convince his fellow workers at the mine that they should stick up for their rights; he was fired for protesting the hiring, firing, promotion, job assignment, and disciplinary policies at the mine; he was fired for standing up to the Anglo bosses who traditionally have looked upon the Chicano much as the southern plantation bigshots have looked upon the Negro. And finally, Joe was fired for his activities outside the mine, where he has dared to stand up to the Corporate Giant, saying, "Your greed stops here, you don't get my land, I've had enough."*
>
> *And when you read the facts of how Manifestly-Destined Anglo America has systematically stolen the land in this part of the country, presuming it has had the God-given right to do the peasants out of everything but their underwear for the past handful of centuries, you begin to realize how these defiant gestures by Joe Cisneros might rankle. So they fired Joe.*

That article was published in May 1970. Though I didn't realize it at the time, Joe Cisneros was a prototype for the kind of person who would become Joe Mondragón, chief protagonist in *The Milagro Beanfield War*. My article dwelled at length on Joe's imaginative struggle to get by. He made hunting knives out of used Skil saw blades and sold them for six bucks a pop; he had fashioned an air compressor out of an old refrigerator motor and a junked sander; he had fabricated a new tractor muffler from a piece of pipe drilled full of holes:

> *And listening to Joe describe his projects and explain how things work, you understand how necessary it is, if you are poor, to learn how to squeeze blood out of a stone. In order to survive you must be able to coddle a machine with spit and baling wire and whatever else is at hand, because often the machine absolutely must function in order for you to eat; and with a little luck and hard work and ingenuity, what other people throw away, the junk in Chicano yards that so offends the tourist from Boston, can keep you going indefinitely.*
>
> *So Joe is not only a highly skilled workman, he is also a man who can work miracles, coaxing an extra four or five lifetimes out of things built to fall apart after two years. And thus deep down, at a most intimate level, Joe is the system's enemy.*

Shortly after the article on Joe Cisneros appeared in the *Review,* I drove to Costilla, a small town on the Colorado border an hour north of Taos. At the time, Costilla was very nearly a ghost town. West of the main highway it was composed largely of ruined old adobes crumbling back into the earth, barren fields, blown-over outhouses, collapsed and splintered roof timbers. East of the highway, pastures were green and

The New Mexico Review — Every Five Days a Hiroshima Bomb Is Dropped On Vietnam (November 1972)

Final issue of the New Mexico Review, featuring my article on the Teatro Campesino, November 1972.

irrigated. I spent but a single afternoon in Costilla; yet the ruins made a lasting impression on me. When I asked a resident about the desolation, she replied vaguely, "Oh, you know, the state took it away. Some people, they had a kind of association, some pull . . . and took all the water. They did it to the poor people . . . it's the poor people who lost the water." Apparently, most of the ruined houses had belonged to bean farmers who departed when they lost their irrigation rights. She smiled: "This used to be a very beautiful place. . . ."

I wrote an article about Costilla, the lost water, the crumbling ghost town. The village became a metaphor that remained in my head. And, although I knew nobody in that town, and did not return to it for years, fictitious Milagro had been born.

Almost every month I contributed a story or two to the *Review.* I wrote about a Chicano-hippy war in Taos, the history of Los Alamos, police brutality. Kit Carson—the patron saint of commercial, tourist Taos (who is often seen by Native Americans as an agent of U.S. genocide)—fell victim to my outraged pen. I supported the Taos pueblo's struggle to recapture its sacred Blue Lake land from the Forest Service. I eulogized Chicano activists murdered by the police, publicized feminist artists, supported a liberal Taos high school social studies course that was derailed by angry parents who denounced it as "socialist." I covered a speech by Reies Tijerina, and documented a visit to New Mexico by Luis Valdez's Teatro Campesino. The Teatro was a political theater group whose raucous, comic style I would eventually try to incorporate into *The Milagro Beanfield War.*

During this time I also did support work for various political groups. One was a cooperative and clinic in Tierra Amarilla, two hours west of me. Another was a Taos organization called Trabajadores de la Raza. I touched down occasionally with a Santa Fe barrio group called La Gente. I remember one fearful night riding police brutality patrols with them. Another time, at a Colorado hospital auction, I purchased beds, lamps, and other supplies for a peoples' clinic opened by La Gente. Often, I went to Española to help in mailings of *El Grito del Norte.* Too, I chronicled water misuse by recreation developers in the Valle Escondido eight miles up Taos Canyon. And I repeatedly criticized the Forest Service grazing and woodcutting policies, which were prejudiced against many longtime residents of the Taos Valley.

One day I drove a carload of old folks from Peñasco down to the Santa Fe legislature for a demonstration against proposed welfare cuts. On the journey south, I chatted with an old man who recounted a wonderful story about his father. I published his tale in the May 1971 *Review:*

*My father now, he's 96 years old, and I got
nine brothers and sisters, all of us living. When
my father was 79, there was a big operation
to save his life. We all thought he was gonna
die. The doctors said he had at the most six
months to live without the operation, maybe
two years or so if the operation was successful.
As a family we had to vote whether the
operation should be done or not. One of my
sisters was sure the operation would kill him,
and voted no. But anyway, they did the
operation, and although he was pretty bad for
a while, he survived. That Christmas my
father called us all together to have a last
celebration, because he didn't think he was
gonna live much longer. So we all came to be
with him on his final Christmas. My brothers
came from California, even, and everybody
said goodbye. Then, when he was 84, the old
man wanted us all to gather again, because
it was gonna be his last Christmas. Well, not
everybody came because not everybody believed
him. Later on, maybe when he was around
90, or something, he wanted all of us to come
again, but a lot of us were too busy, and
besides, by then who believed him anyway? He
was real sickly when he was a child, and he's
been sick a lot all his life. Just a couple of years
ago he was operated on again, and I was sure
when I looked at him in that hospital that he
wasn't going to walk out of there. But he did,
and he can still read the newspapers. . . .*

In *Milagro* that story became the foundation
for an indestructible character, Amarante
Córdova, whom I saw also as a metaphor
for a culture that refused to die.

In fact, it was the old-timers around Taos
who most clearly conveyed to me a sense
of the land, the agricultural rhythm of life,
the culture, politics, and economics of the
valley. Granted, I worked with many people
my own age on various projects — organizers
like Kelly Lovato, Jerry Ortiz y Pino;
progressive lawyers like Peggy Nelson and
Tony López, or like the Taos enjarradora,
Anita Rodríguez. I visited Tierra Amarilla
a few times in support of clinic functions put
together by folks like Maria Varela and
Moises Morales and Dr. Ed Bernstein, or La
Raza Unida members Ike De Vargas and his
hardworking mouthpiece, Richard
Rosenstock. I attended benefits in support
of the Ensenada Velásquez family, which was

Craig Vincent, the best of the old-time organizers.

Craig Vincent, the best of the old-time organizers.

defending its land against an attempted takeover by a Rio Arriba ski area developer. I wrote an article on their principal spokesman, Esteben Polaco, whose determination to protect his family's roots had a lot in common with my friend Joe Cisneros — and the fictional Joe Mondragón.

But the old-timers most powerfully gifted to me the Taos Valley. Some, like my immediate neighbors, Eloy Pacheco and Bernardo Trujillo, taught me the lore and structure of the two irrigation ditches running through my property. Another, Melitón Trujillo, who lived across the river from my house, talked about old-time politics and sang corridos he had invented during Republican-Democrat frays of old. Jim Suazo, at the Taos pueblo, was a dignified and powerful storyteller; his son-in-law, George Track, was a loquacious Sioux adventurer whose extended family and convoluted, cliff-hanging lifestyle always touched me deeply.

Most especially I learned from two men: Craig Vincent — an organizer from the small village of San Cristobal, fifteen minutes north of Taos, — and Andrés Martínez — a former sheep shearer, Indian trading post manager, and small dairy farmer in Taos. Craig died in the summer of 1985. Andrés, at 87, is still spry and very much involved in the politics of this valley.

Craig was a formal political man and Marxist theorist. In the late sixties and early seventies his political wisdom, knowledge of bookkeeping, and tireless fundraising kept the Tierra Amarilla Clinic alive — it is now one of the premier health care facilities in northern New Mexico. Craig also supported the Crusade for Justice in Denver. In Taos, he established a chapter of the U.S.-China Peoples' Friendship Committee, of which I was a member. Craig helped the *New Mexico Review,* and my guess is that at one time or another, his gentle, wise, and articulate hand must have touched almost every socially concerned group in New Mexico. The ACLU gave him its prestigious Civil Libertarian award; the Tierra Amarilla Clinic named its largest building after Craig. He fought against the war in Vietnam, and later denounced the misuse of grand juries in the United States. I often met him at events protesting U.S. policies in Central America. We participated in political study groups together. Craig was a low-key, committed man with impeccable integrity, a wonderful sense of humor, and great love for northern New Mexico and the world.

Andrés Martínez entered my life in 1970, when Taos was slated for a conservancy district and a large water impoundment project to be made possible by construction of the Indian Camp Dam. Andrés presided over a coalition of valley acequias against the dam, called the Tres Rios Association. Older men allied with Andrés, who also became my friends, were Paul Valerio, Bernabé Chávez, J. J. García, Jacob Bernal, Pacomio Mondragón.

For years I worked with the Tres Rios Association while it fought the conservancy and the dam. People protested because the socioeconomic changes to be triggered by the enormous development project would threaten the valley's marginal citizens— mostly Spanish-speaking small farmers

This poster, designed by Rini Templeton, was used to raise money for the Tres Rios Association.

unable (and unwilling) to compete with high-pressure capitalist ventures.

Tres Rios meetings were the best education I could have gotten about the social structure, personality, and history of Taos. I also did research for Legal Aid lawyers working on the case. In the process, I learned more about land and water rights history than I could ever have dreamed possible. I also drew cartoons for newspaper ads against the dam, and designed flyers to protest it or to call the public to meetings. Upon occasion I hiked from one end of Taos to the other, leafleting automobiles with yet another anti-conservancy call to arms. At one point I had the State Engineer's hydrographic survey maps of the entire Taos Valley pinned to the walls of my kitchen, living room, and bedroom as part of an effort to learn the landholding patterns of the entire valley. I spent hours in the county courthouse researching titles, attempting to discover the true ownership behind dummy corporations.

And I wrote about the Indian Camp Dam controversy for the *New Mexico Review.* In the July 1972 issue, I summed up the problem like so:

Leaders of the Taos anti-conservancy struggle, 1972 (L-R): Amadeo Valerio, Paul Valerio, Andrés Martínez, Pacomio Mondragón, Polito Martínez, and Legal Aid lawyer, Gene Weisfeld.

The fact is, the history of Conservancy disasters in New Mexico, in which the small Chicano farmer has always been the fall guy, is lengthy and depressing. It can be summed up in these words from noted sociologist Dr. Clark Knowlton: "Every major irrigation or water conservation project along the Rio Grande River, from the Elephant Butte Dam to the Middle Rio Grande Conservancy District, has been responsible for land alienation on an extensive scale. The Spanish-Americans have been replaced by Anglo-American farmers. Their subsistence agriculture has made way for a highly commercial, partially subsidized, and basically insecure agriculture made possible by government programs. Little thought has ever been given to the rights and land use patterns of the Spanish-Americans in planning water projects in New Mexico and in neighboring states."

It was a classic battle of the big boys versus the little guys. Allied against the Taos small farmers were the State Engineer, Steve Reynolds, and his right-hand gunslinger, Paul Bloom (whom I repeatedly jabbed at

Nichols '72

Bloom doesn't know what to do with the Indian Camp Dam.

with *Review* cartoons). The Bureau of Reclamation was eager to build the dam. Most realtors, bankers, lawyers, motel and hotel owners of Taos favored the project. All the money was stacked on the side of progress, American style. Yet Andrés Martínez and his cohorts, who began with almost no precedent, no money, and no political power on their side, ultimately defeated the conservancy district and the Indian Camp Dam.

To me, the Taos conservancy struggle was a lot like the 1950s film *Salt of the Earth*, which I first saw at Em Hall's house in Pecos. The movie is about a successful miners' strike in southern New Mexico. It not only treats Chicanos and working class people with respect, but it is also a powerful feminist film, and was long banned or suppressed in this country because of its "communist sympathies." Later, when I wrote *The Milagro Beanfield War*, I hoped that I could emulate successfully the message and the humanity of that film.

So I discovered the history of Taos

Paul Bloom, special assistant to the State Engineer, confronts a Taos small farmer.

Nichols '72

through Craig Vincent, Andrés Martínez, and their friends. I learned about community complexities, the feuds, the intricate and extended family ties, the political shenanigans. Most importantly, I absorbed my neighbors' ties to the lands, and participated in their—in our—struggle to defend it.

Meantime, as the *Review* floundered toward its November 1972 extinction, I did some personal floundering of my own. I had published *The Sterile Cuckoo* in 1965, *The Wizard of Loneliness* in 1966. After that, my literature became so infused with political rage that I hadn't published a thing. I was thirty-two and money was scarce—almost nonexistent. My marriage was on the rocks. The mortgage on my four-room adobe house was only $78.38 a month, but I often had trouble making the payments. I heated with wood, used an outhouse, and didn't even have a car. It looked like curtains for the not-so-young-anymore writer whom H. Allen Smith once suggested in print "will likely become the best comic novel writer of his time. . . ."

Truth to tell, I didn't feel very funny anymore. I was torn between trying to write polemical books, or just ditching my artistic pretensions and gravitating toward more immediate political barricades.

In the end, I chose to give political literature a final shot. What followed has become slightly apocryphal—at least in my eyes. During one of our hellacious hockey matches in Albuquerque, I told Em Hall the *Review* was dead, I could not afford to edit it any longer. He passed the puck anyway, and I scored a few more goals. Then I sat down and began a new book on a one-sentence premise: a 35-year-old unemployed Chicano handyman named José Mondragón (who was about as desperate as myself) cuts water illegally into a half-acre beanfield, and all hell breaks loose. Eventually, his act goads a community of impoverished, working-class people to organize against a big dam and recreation development (made possible by a conservancy district) that threatens to wipe them out.

The kitchen was freezing, so I typed fast on my little Hermes Rocket to keep warm. I churned out the first 500-page draft of *The Milagro Beanfield War* in five weeks. I took three more weeks to correct it, another three weeks retyping the book. At that point the Hermes collapsed, I chucked it into the trash, and sent the book off to my agent, Perry Knowlton at Curtis Brown in New York. By then it was the end of January 1973. Perry gave the book to Marian Wood, an editor at Holt, Rinehart & Winston, and

Taos small farmers hogtie Bloom. Cartoons like these appeared often in the **New Mexico Review.**

Nichols '72

13

New Mexico always seemed like a third world, or colonial country . . . and my cartoons often pointed this out.

Marian promptly bought the book for 10Gs. I was astonished. Only four months had passed from the start to the score.

After the long famine such a sudden feast!

Then I scrambled to rewrite the book. Holt gave me eight more months to "tinker." While I was tinkering, producer-actor Tony Bill dropped by Curtis Brown and asked, "Anything new from John Nichols?" (Tony is a guardian angel who gave my first novel, *The Sterile Cuckoo,* to Liza Minelli, who starred in Alan Pakula's film version, which kept me passably alive from 1966 until I came up empty in 1972.) Perry handed Tony a second draft *Milagro* manuscript, and Tony gave the manuscript to his friends Bob Christiansen and Rick Rosenberg, producers of "The Autobiography of Miss Jane Pittman." They liked it, got in touch with the Curtis Brown film agent, Richard Parks, and all of a sudden *Milagro* was out on option eight months before publication! Plans were to hire Mark Medoff, of "When You Comin Back Red Ryder?" fame, to do the script. Tomorrow Entertainment would spring for the development bread. Boy, what a reversal of my fortunes!

Of course, Hollywood has long been a reactionary industry which generally has treated minority people in a patronizing or downright racist manner. A good reason, I initially surmised, never to let *Milagro* out on option. Aside from rare films like *Salt of the Earth, Zoot Suit,* or *The Ballad of Gregorio Cortéz,* the traditional image of Chicanos and Latinos has been either as thugs, as the

14

butts of dope and toilet jokes, or as quasi-morons obsessed with gang warfare and hydraulics.

Nevertheless, as a film freak from age seven, I have always understood that good films *do* get made. And so my idealist side believed a *Milagro* film could break the worst Hollywood stereotypes. Still, it was a risky adventure. If the outcome was patronizing, all option and other payments I'd taken would seem like blood money in the worst sense. But if the film had a political and cultural integrity, then, hopefully, it would count in the struggle of all peoples to assert their basic human rights.

Unfortunately, after writing an outline of *Milagro,* Mark Medoff disappeared into the convolutions of his theater world and proceeded no further on the script. Chris-Rose left Tomorrow Entertainment. Meantime, *Milagro* was published to fairly good reviews and a semi-resounding commercial clunk. Holt did a small second printing, but then abruptly remaindered the book.

I was broke again, but I invested $200 to buy some 400 hardback copies of the novel, and I passed them out like canapés to any friend, foe, fan, or local bookstore that was interested. I thought I'd have hardback copies for the rest of my life; instead, within months all my originals were gone.

At the last minute, paperback rights sold to Ballantine for $7,500 — so, financially, I was saved by the bell. Fresh off that triumph, for $40 I bought another Hermes Rocket — the world's last, great disposable typewriter — and churned out two more novels, both of which were immediately rejected. And very shortly I was right back where I had started in 1972.

To Bob Christiansen and Rick Rosenberg, who kept renewing the *Milagro* option, I owed my survival. By 1975 Paramount was fronting the development bread. Chris-Rose hired Tracy Keenan Wynn, the author of "Miss Jane Pittman," to write the *Milagro* script, and I was ecstatic. What could go wrong now?

Well, time passed quickly — 1976, 1977. Chris-Rose persistently renewed the *Milagro* option, which kept the project *and* me alive. My literary career was dead again; I was struggling with a novel called *The Magic Journey.* While I stumbled toward completion of that new book, *Variety* announced that Paramount would soon be filming *Milagro.* But Tracy's script of the novel had problems. Biggest one, no doubt, was trying to distill a 600-page novel with some 200 characters down into a two-hour "ensemble" piece, in which at least half the characters spoke Spanish as their primary language.

Though I'm a novelist at heart, I've long believed in the axiom that to make a film, "you buy the book and throw it away." Here, however, we were also dealing with executives whose initial reaction to the project was, "Who wants to see a movie about a bunch of Mexicans?" Particularly a bunch of Mexicans who took on the traditional Anglo power structure, winning a victory that went completely against the grain of progress, American style. Too, the moneymen wanted a "star" attached to the movie. A Chicano star? Not at all. They were talking Al Pacino, Dustin Hoffman, Robert de Niro: I cringed.

So the project never really caught fire. Tracy's script receded into the background, Lorimar stepped in to take over the development financing, and Leonard Gardner, of *Fat City* fame, tackled a new screenplay. *Hollywood Reporter* announced that Lorimar would soon start filming *Milagro.* Warren Bayless, my new film agent at Curtis Brown, advised me not to hold my breath.

During this time, on the home front, the Indian Camp Dam battle continued. A district judge formed the conservancy district in Taos. The Tres Rios Association appealed that decision to the state supreme court. And, on a technicality, the supreme court overturned the district decision,

Almost every year, from 1974 to 1986, somebody somewhere announced the filming of Milagro.

Movie of Novel To Be Made Here

By HUGH GALLAGHER
Journal Entertainment Writer

A film version of John Nichols' novel "The Milagro Beanfield War" will be shot in New Mexico late this summer.

Larry Hamm, director of the film division of the New Mexico Department of Development, said the film will be produced by Chris Rose and Lorimar Productions. Lorimar does many movies for television and "The Waltons" television series. "The Milagro Beanfield War" will be a feature film for theaters.

Nichols' novel concerns water disputes in northern New Mexico. Hamm said the producers are negotiating with a name actor to star.

Hamm said the ABC television series "How The West Was Won" will be shooting for eight weeks in New Mexico beginning in June.

"Alacran," a $2.5 million film being produced by Markham Productions, will be shooting in Las Cruces from May to July.

The long-delayed Ray Stark production, "The Electric Horseman" will be shot later this year under the direction of Sidney Pollack.

Already announced for this year are two major theatrical productions and several smaller productions. Production has already begun on 20th Century-Fox prequel to "Butch Cassidy and the Sundance Kid." Hamm said the company has been shooting snow scenes in the mountains. Martin Ransohoff's production of "Nightwing" will begin shooting in April.

The British Broadcasting Company is working on pre-production for a documentary on the Navajos.

The multi-million dollar "Superman" production is doing second unit photography in Lamy, Gallup and Santa Fe.

Hamm announced that several other movie companies are considering New Mexico for location shooting. EMI is interested in shooting "The Last Gun" in Las Vegas. Other prospects are Quinn Martin's "The Hidden Earth," Marjoe Gortner's production of Mark Medoff's "When You Comin' Back Red Ryder" and American International's "The Muddy Ball."

throwing out the conservancy district. I'll wager that this was one of the few times in modern southwestern history, that a people as poor and politically "powerless" as the Taos farmers had managed to organize successfully against a state- and federally-supported irrigation project of such magnitude.

Life imitates the art that imitated life!

Regarding the movies, Leonard Gardner's *Milagro* script wound up lacking energy. It was rewritten umpteen times; yet despite the best of intentions it eventually became obvious that this effort was also doomed. *The Magic Journey* was published, went

nowhere. And, as the winter of 1978 approached, I was broke and cold once more, desperately flailing away on a new novel, *A Ghost in the Music,* and a non-fiction book, *If Mountains Die.*

When it was published, *If Mountains Die* featured beautiful color photographs of the Taos Valley by my friend Bill Davis. The book is gentle compared to *Magic Journey.* Yet at many levels — and particularly because of Bill's evocative photographs — I felt that it made a strong political statement. Though no slogans clutter Bill's serene landscapes, I learned from the success of our book that beauty itself is an effective weapon in the battle to revere and protect life.

The year *If Mountains Die* came out (1979), I began packing a camera on all excursions about my home territory. In the process, I soon realized that all landscape (and photographs of it) is defined by human attitudes and sensibilities. In particular, all Taos scenes I witnessed seemed powerfully connected to the legacies of cultures which have dominated the valley for centuries. Because nature is essentially at our mercy, each beautiful landscape I photographed seemed to praise the human history of this place.

When the *Milagro* option expired in 1979, Bob and Rick were broke and exhausted after their six-year struggle — they gave up. It made me sad because they were good men who tried hard. Several interested parties waited in the wings, however. By then *Milagro* had become what some literary pundits were calling "an underground cult classic." The original hardbacks, that I had once so cavalierly given away, were now going for $40 to $60 a pop. My new Curtis Brown film agent, Tim Knowlton (who was eighteen in 1973 when this process began), mentioned that Robert Redford's office had extended a nibble. Cheech Marin had also made faint noises. A consortium of Albuquerque business people got in touch, apparently interested in a big-time tax shelter.

John Nichols (behind wheel), Bill Davis, and Bill's truck, Zeke, circa 1978. Photograph by William Davis.

One afternoon I found myself in an Albuquerque Sheraton downing beers with a man named Moctesuma Esparza. He was soft-spoken, peered disarmingly out at the world through thick-lensed glasses, and had made only one film that I knew of, a lovely documentary short on a Medenales, New Mexico, weaver named Agueda Martínez; it had been nominated for an Academy Award. Mocte seemed to have little money or clout, which immediately endeared him to me. He had been active in the Chicano movement, which made me like him even better.

The plan was to obtain a NEH grant, in conjunction with the National Council of La Raza, to start the picture. It would begin as a small-time project geared toward PBS. I would write a script for the Writers Guild minimum. Once we had a script, we'd try to raise major theatrical interest, get a studio involved, and go for a feature film.

Moctesuma and the National Council of La Raza received the bucks to proceed . . . and then my phone rang—it was Robert Redford, interested in the *Milagro* option. Though I explained that Esparza owned it, Bob wanted to visit Taos anyway. By then it was spring 1980, and I was fairly jaded. I was much more involved in cleaning out the ditches again, planting the garden, gearing up to face another summer of hysterical fecundity.

In due course Redford called once more. This time he was at a Hudson gas station in Taos, and he was pissed because he'd just been ticketed for speeding while entering town. He had tried to argue his way out of it, but the cop merely smiled and admitted he'd never ticketed a movie star before.

I drove in, met Bob, led him home. We talked at the kitchen table while my kids and various neighbor children peeped in the windows. I reiterated what I'd already explained: Esparza really *did* own the option. Bob laughed: "You mean I drove all the way here for nothing?" I suggested, "Well, you could always talk with Mocte about it." And he departed after cheerfully posing with my

17

ten-year-old daughter, Tania, and two neighbor friends for a photograph that would decorate their walls for years to come.

Months passed. I futzed with a new novel, *The Nirvana Blues* (for which I could not even hustle an advance). Esparza gave no go-ahead to commence a script. He and Bob were talking. Eventually, they decided to work together and signed a joint venture agreement. So now it was Redford with whom I would discuss the script. But Bob had more or less disappeared . . . so finally, as winter approached, I took a deep breath and blammed out a "preliminary" draft screenplay. I considered it a rough document to be used simply for talking points. Hopefully, it would generate reactions so that finally we could proceed.

Mostly, my awkward script generated a big silence.

No matter. By then, quite suddenly, I had other fish to fry. It all began with another of those mysterious phone calls. This time a producer named Eddie Lewis asked if I would come to L.A. to meet Costa-Gavras

and talk about rewriting a film. *Costa-Gavras?* Back then I was terrified of planes, so I trained out to Los Angeles. A limousine driver handed me a script of the film that would eventually be called *Missing*. Slouched way down so that nobody I might know would spy me riding in that symbol of bourgeois decadence, I read the script on my way to the Marina Pacific Hotel in Venice. Costa and I palavered for three days. Then I was given three weeks to rewrite the script. I asked for six weeks—no deal. How about five?—huh-uh. "Listen," I whined, blurting out the old Hollywood joke: "I'm real new at this, so do you want it great, or do you want it by Tuesday?" They wanted it by Tuesday. That meant January 15, 1981.

Hollywood! I had almost no "track record," and not the slightest idea of what I was doing. But in three weeks I returned the rewritten script. Everyone was apparently ecstatic. *Missing* got made. It garnered four Academy Award nominations, and actually won one for Best Adapted Screenplay. But by then I had been arbitrated out of a screen credit by my own union, the Writers Guild. I launched reams of nasty letters to Writers Guild president, Frank Pierson *(Cat Ballou, Dog Day Afternoon)*, trashing him and his organization for cashiering my credit.

Nevertheless, the success of *Missing* gave me a bit more confidence to work on *Milagro.* Especially, I had a renewed faith that the political film was alive and well in America.

My initial *Milagro* script was not great shakes—heavy on the sight gags, pretty loose on construction. Bob suggested we now work on it together at Sundance in Utah, during the first annual Film Institute there. He would be in one place for an entire month, and was eager to get started. Me, too.

Then the Writers Guild went out on strike. I was dumbfounded—*what schmucks!* But, unelated as I might have felt about losing my *Missing* credit, I believe in unions and would never cross a picket line. So I would not even chat casually about *Milagro,* let alone touch pencil to paper in search of a better script.

Frantically, during the strike, I churned out a non-fiction book called *The Last Beautiful Days of Autumn,* and scored a modest advance. Bob invited me to Sundance for a week, anyway, as a gesture of friendship. I could watch films being made, maybe learn something.

I went, and it was a fascinating and turbulent week during which nobody even mentioned *Milagro.* Shortly after I departed Sundance, the strike was settled. But by then Redford was out there in seventy-two different places at once—to all intents and purposes he had disappeared again. And Mocte was busy cranking up his new film, *The Ballad of Gregorio Cortéz.* Plus I was flying around the country on a book tour for *The Nirvana Blues,* and also trying to prepare the *Autumn* book for 1982 publication. Too, I was doing an original script for Costa-Gavras on the daily lives of nuclear physicists.

So *I* had disappeared to boot!

The next few years were crazy. By the end of December 1982, I'd written several *Milagro* scripts for Esparza and Redford. To help me out, they hired Frank Pierson (the Writers Guild prexy whom I'd castigated repeatedly for my lost *Missing* credit) to work with me on the *Milagro* project. Small world. Turned out Frank and I liked each other. I forgave him the guild's trespasses, he forgave me my poison-pen letters, and we spent some good times together in Taos hacking away on the script. The Hollywood trades suggested that Redford would soon start filming *Milagro.* Instead, none of my scripts captured anyone's imagination, and the project, as far as I could tell, puttered off into idleness.

By then I was too busy on other fronts to truly notice. From 1982 until well into 1985, I worked on several different screen projects: another with Costa-Gavras based on a post-nuclear war novel called *Warday;* I also did a rough first draft of *The Magic Journey* for Louis Malle. And, with Karel Reisz, I wrote a screenplay dealing with Haitian refugees, the U.S. Coast Guard, and moral decisions which override unjust laws.

In early 1985, when I was finally dropped from *Warday,* I returned to literature with a great sigh of relief, finished off a non-fiction book called *On the Mesa,* and started a new novel, *American Blood.* At some point around then I learned Redford and Esparza had hired David Ward, Bob's writer on *The Sting,* to do yet another *Milagro* script. Then, suddenly, a draft of Ward's product appeared in my mailbox. When I read it, my heart sank. Its punch line was that a Chicano farmer doesn't know the difference between peas and pinto beans, so he accidentally plants and nurtures a field of peas, thinking they are beans. No such lunacy darkens any page of my novel. And I thought: Oh dear, if *Milagro* is actually filmed according to *this* plot line, now is probably as good a time as ever to commit suicide!

Instead, after living alone for a decade, I married a beautiful woman named Juanita

Wolf, and together we went jogging off into the sunset on the mesa west of Taos.

Later, Juanita and I came down to earth and went back to work, together. Part of that work meant attending dozens of meetings called to protest the ongoing "pizzification" of the Taos Valley. As things had been in 1970 when I began writing for the *Review,* so they were still in 1985. Meetings to control rafting on the Rio Grande, thereby preserving the delicate ecology of the Wild River Gorge. Meetings to stop a highway bypass that might destroy the last pure agricultural land around. Meetings to challenge the government's 50-year plan for the Carson National Forest (which comprises 44% of Taos County). Meetings to prevent the Questa moly mine from building a new tailings pond whose effluence could pollute the Rio Grande. . . .

By the spring of 1986, it seemed Robert Redford was actually going to direct *The*

Milagro Beanfield War. Variety, the New Mexico Film Commission, and the Albuquerque *Journal* all claimed it was true. The more that rumors flew, the less I believed them. The *Milagro* film project had

Another blistering Nichols portrayal of Smokey the Bear, controversial symbol of the U.S. Forest Service.

20

become a celluloid Amarante Cordova that refused to get made, even as it also refused to die.

A production manager named David Wisnievitz arrived in Taos: we had breakfast at Michael's Café. David was scouting locations. *Milagro* actually . . . almost . . . just about for sure . . . looked like a "go" picture. And the peas had been changed back to beans. *That* was a relief! But I still figured the odds were a million to one against it. And I was broke again, so I took another film job, a six-hour TV miniseries on the life of Pancho Villa and the Mexican Revolution.

When Bob next called, he informed me that Universal planned to front the ten-million epic, and would I do a fast polish of the script? Of course I would. Juanita and I traveled to Sundance, meeting with Bob and an assistant, Sarah Black, for three days in June. Back in Taos, over two horrible, manic weeks, I churned out a polish of David Ward's script. Shades of *Missing!* I *had* to finish the thing by Tuesday.

Exhausted, I completed the script, and a courier arrived to grab my work and pouch it off immediately to Bob. I expected an instantaneous reaction, then more day-night frantic working sessions to bang it into shape before filming started. Instead, the script disappeared out there, and I heard next to nothing for three weeks: no phone calls, utter silence, zilch. I couldn't worry about it too much, however, because by then I was frantically trying to produce a "bible" for the Pancho Villa films.

Soon the starting day for the *Milagro* shoot loomed just two weeks away. All the New Mexico papers flaunted the *Milagro* follies. Just north of Santa Fe lies a small town, Chimayo, where the main sets were to be built. But at the last minute, Chimayo rejected the movie. Residents of the old plaza claimed the movie would shatter their privacy. And for a moment it looked as if the project might collapse. Instead, the entire operation relocated in another, more remote,

village called Truchas.

Of course, Truchas is perched at 8,500 feet, where the first snow is liable to fall on August 15th! Oblivious to such facts, the set makers started all over, with orders to build Rome in a day. In late July I asked David Wisnievitz how it was all going. He replied, "No problem." Considering that the shoot must begin in two weeks, that they had not even half finished the Truchas sets, that there was no cast as yet, that the script was a total question mark, and that nobody really knew where Redford *was* . . . things couldn't have been more hunky-dory.

Incredibly, Bob finally appeared, rented a house in Santa Fe, and began filming *The Milagro Beanfield War* two months later than it should have started, and still without a cast. I did a hasty polish of a script compiled by Sarah Black (and a fellow named Jim Parks) out of former versions by David Ward and myself. I understood that another writer on the set was doing an all-new, computerized version. Frankly, I was a trifle befuddled by all the chaos surrounding the launching of such a mammoth enterprise.

Milagro was as difficult for Redford to hobble as a goat.

Redford on the set with Chic Vennera as Joe Mondragón.

But by then I was so busy editing my new novel, and slaving away on Pancho Villa, that I couldn't worry much about *Milagro.*

Though Bob moved slowly at first, the dailies Juanita and I saw were full of life and humor. The actors and crew were very friendly the few times we managed to visit the set. The eleventh-hour cast was varied, rich, funky, cheerful: Chic Vennera, Ruben Blades, Christopher Walken, Trinidad Silva, Daniel Stern, John Heard, Sonia Braga, Julie Carmen, Freddy Fender, James Gammon, Melanie Griffith, Carlos Riquelme, Robert Carricart . . . ad infinitum. Fifty-three speaking parts! My favorite was a local Santa Fe woman whom Redford apparently just spotted on the street. Her name is Julia García and she plays a daffy old lady, Mercedes Rael, who flings pebbles at everybody. She seemed absolutely perfect.

By October I had grown quite complacent about the whole process. Then—*boom!* On October 22, the producers of a film about the life of land grant activist Reies Tijerina, to be called *King Tiger,* filed suit against the *Milagro* film, against Redford,

and against script writer David Ward, claiming that *Milagro* was based on Tijerina's life. They wanted an injunction against the continued filming of *Milagro.* They claimed our film had caused Columbia to shelve *King Tiger.*

Naturally, I was flabbergasted. José Mondragón, a 35-year-old unemployed handyman who cuts water illegally into a half-acre beanfield bore some kind of resemblance to an evangelical preacher who became the messianic leader of a land grant movement that climaxed in an armed raid on the Tierra Amarilla, New Mexico, courthouse in 1967? Wow! It had to be a joke. A bad joke. Though my book had often been vilified in the fourteen years since its publication, no one had ever suggested it was based even remotely on Tijerina.

Neither I nor the book (at the date of this writing) were being sued. But I was rendered nearly catatonic by visions of negative publicity: for Tijerina, for myself, for *Milagro,* for the whole effort to create a project with dignity, with political and cultural integrity. It was an insult to all my friends, and to all the local struggles which had inspired the novel.

That night, reporters phoned for my reaction. I could think of nothing to comment except that the whole thing was

Freddy Fender and Daniel Stern on the **Milagro** *set.*

Tijerina Sues To Stop 'Milagro' Filming

FROM STAFF AND WIRE REPORTS

SANTA FE — Land grant activist Reies Lopez Tijerina and a movie producer filed a lawsuit Wednesday in an effort to halt production of director Robert Redford's "The Milagro Beanfield War."

The suit, filed in federal court in Los Angeles, claims the movie is based on Tijerina's activities during the middle 1960s and alleges copyright violation and invasion of privacy.

The suit seeks unspecified damage awards and an injunction to halt production of the Universal Studios movie, currently being filmed in Northern New Mexico.

Redford said through a spokesman Wednesday: "This is typical. It happens on every film. Somebody comes out of the woodwork with their hand out."

The suit says that "Silkwood" producer Robert Cano and his Pisces Productions own the rights to the story of Tijerina's life and his confrontation with the government over land rights, which Cano planned to produce with a script titled "King Tiger."

Columbia Pictures, however, has shelved plans for "King Tiger" because Redford is producing

Reies Lopez Tijerina
Land grant activist

Robert Redford
Director of "Milagro"

John Nichols
Author of "Milagro"

"Milagro," Cano claims.

Neither the 1974 book "The Milagro Beanfield War" by Taos author John Nichols nor the movie on which it is based uses the name of Tijerina.

However, attorneys for the Coyote, N.M., resident and Cano say the book and script for the movie

are clearly based on Tijerina's activities and that the motion picture being directed by Redford defames Tijerina.

Nichols' novel tells a comical story of a feisty Hispanic who defies the establishment, including a wealthy Anglo land developer, in a rebellion over water rights.

Reached for comment on the suit late Wednesday, Nichols said, "I

to honor Spanish land grants he said were part of a century-old treaty.

Tijerina, who served 30 months in prison for incidents related to his attempted takeover of government-owned land in 1965, said he was trying to force the U.S. government

think it's sad, that's all."

Both Nichols and Redford's spokesman said they were waiting to see the lawsuit before making any further comment. "I would be nuts to comment until I see it," said Nichols.

Reid Rosefelt, publicist for Redford's production company, said filming of "Milagro" is still under way in Truchas and that the crew hopes to finish in early November.

Also named as defendants in the suit are scriptwriter David Ward, Redford's Wildwood Productions and co-producer Moctesuma Esparza's Esparza Productions.

"Mr. Tijerina is clearly the pivotal point in the entire drama of the modern New Mexico land grant conflict, which culminated in the courthouse raid at Tierra Amarilla," attorney Federico Sayre wrote in an Oct. 7 letter to Universal Motion Picture President Sean Daniel.

That same letter claims "Milagro" scriptwriter Ward was shown the treatment for Cano's "King Tiger," and said he was interested in doing the film writing.

"Ward told us he would like to write the (screen)play, if he could direct," Sayre said Wednesday. Universal, which purchased

movie rights to the Nichols book, refused comment on the lawsuit Wednesday, keeping with company policy not to discuss matters in litigation, spokesman Allan Sutton said.

Tijerina, who sold the rights to his story to Cano, claims he has suffered invasion of privacy, defamation and financial loss because he will be associated with "Milagro" and because Columbia's decision to shelve "King Tiger" caused him to lose his percentage of prospective net profit on the project.

A spokesman for Tijerina's family in Coyote said Wednesday that Tijerina currently is in Spain and won't return until the end of the month.

Tijerina told the Journal in a December 1984 interview that he had signed a contract with Cano on his life, in which he insisted that his real name be used. Tijerina also said he required that "King Tiger" be presented as a truthful account, using real names and places.

Neither Cano, who lives in Pasadena, Calif., nor Tijerina disclosed what Tijerina would be paid for his story and his services as an adviser through all phases of the movie.

---

absurd. Privately, I believed the suit was a tragedy. I figured the upcoming scandal would undermine a trust I felt I'd built up over seventeen years of organizing in, and writing about, northern New Mexico. I wished to tell reporters: "To say *Milagro* is based on Reies Tijerina is like saying Walt Disney's *Pinocchio* is based on the life of Christ." Fortunately, I managed to keep my mouth shut.

Still, I envisioned a thousand obscene repercussions against which I'd be helpless to act. No doubt, the suit would be the most offensive intrusion on my life — and on my work — that I had ever experienced.

But nothing happened. Gory details were announced to the press, but the legal papers, so far, anyway, have not been served. After one day the newspapers dropped the story. They picked it up briefly, a month later, when Tijerina pulled out of the suit. Then all fell silent again. And *Milagro* continued filming as if the suit didn't exist. Once again, Amarante Córdova had refused to die!

Came finally the last day of the shoot. Good friend Victoria Plata, who handled extras on the film, asked Juanita to be in the scene. We stumbled out of bed at 5 A.M. and slouched down the highway to Santa Fe in a pickup that skidded dangerously on sheer ice — it had just snowed eighteen inches! Bad weather had held up production by more than a month.

We spent a long day in the posh living room of a ritzy house just north of Santa Fe. Mostly, we waited around. Dozens of huge semi trucks got stuck on the narrow, muddy roads leading to the house. An army of technicians tromped about in muddy moon boots and puffy ski jackets, laying down a million miles of wires, setting up klieg lights and gelatin sheets, and in general destroying the lovely house and its pretty grounds.

The scene was supposed to take place in summertime. Half the extras had frostbite on their toes. The shoot lasted from 10 A.M. to 9 P.M. Juanita stood around looking radiant, sipping apple juice "champagne,"

The last kind of publicity I ever expected, or desired.

23

Juanita Nichols and Debbie Martínez, last day of shooting, November 1986.

Chiricahua Mountains . . . and nearly thirty years later a famous actor directs a movie whose roots travel back to that bewitching summer. Did I write *Milagro* and the other books excerpted here for the same reasons that Esparza and Redford risked more than ten million dollars to launch the film? Probably not. *Milagro,* and my other work, is inspired by a radical political dream which is not often touted in our culture. Yet, hopefully, the film will reflect honorably upon the land and the people who work it, not just in Taos or in New Mexico, but everywhere. I figure if the film can hold even half a candle to *Salt of the Earth,* to Andrés Martínez, or to the values of a man like Craig Vincent, it will make me very happy indeed.

I have been grateful for Redford's pronouncements to the media. On November 2, 1986, the Philadelphia *Inquirer* quoted Bob as follows:

loving every minute. I reacted more wearily: How did such a ponderous operation ever accomplish *anything? Eighty thousand dollars a day?* Imagine if I could send that loot in medical supplies to the Sandinistas! Many times the mariachi band of Debbie Martínez — La Chicanita — struck up its peppy music for the cameras, and that helped keep people awake. Redford chewed gum and stayed in remarkably good humor through it all. Some crew members were real glad it was almost over, however: recently, graffiti had sprung up around Santa Fe — "Free the Milagro 100!"

By day's end, some extras grumbled that it was a lot harder than they had ever thought it could be. But not Juanita. She looked more ebullient at 9 P.M. than she had at ten that morning. Hey, she actually had been directed by Robert Redford! And from now on her bags would be packed, just waiting for Hollywood to call.

Yes, Virginia, there really *is* some glamour in making movies after all!

What, then, remains as the moral of this story?

In 1957, a boy wanders among the

> *First,* **Milagro** *is about the little guys against the big guys. Second,* **Milagro** *also addresses the issue of responsible land use, which is an interest of mine. A point that developers don't always see is that their new projects often threaten to eradicate indigenous culture. If this goes on unchecked, places that have distinct ethnic and architectural heritages are in danger of being homogenized, being like every place else. It's not widely known that the Hispanic community in this valley has a . . . history predating Plymouth Rock, and the Indian community three times that. And that's the third reason it's exciting for me to work on* **Milagro.** *Like* **Jeremiah Johnson,** *it teaches history in an entertaining way. I think there's a suspicion among many Americans that the peoples of northern New Mexico are not real citizens. The truth is, they were here long before us Anglos. My criticism of this country — particularly under the Reagan administration — is that we're ignorant of history and other culture, and I think* **Milagro** *might help to correct that cultural ignorance.*

Andrés Martínez confronts illegal sprinkling (of a resort golf course) which deprives Taos small farmers of their irrigation water, August 1972.

In that, and other statements, Redford has expressed some of my own hopes for the impact of my work. In the following five-part essay, which is constructed entirely of excerpts taken from my writings since 1974, I have sought to present personal experiences and impressions in a way that is true to the rhythm of this wonderful country. My journey in Taos, like that of any explorer, began with the magic of first impressions, as recorded in *On the Brink of Oceans.* Subsequently, I immersed myself in the weather, landscape, seasons—the local *Cycles of Life.* That led inevitably to friendships with, and respect for, my neighbors and my community, as depicted in *The People . . . Yes.* Of course, once committed to both the natural and the human landscape, a person cannot help but develop a concern for his or her community's present and future health, hence, *A Future Up for Grabs.* Finally, conscience demands that we *all* protect what is hallowed, and that is the simple message of the concluding section here—*We Shall Advance Together.*

I trust that in the *Milagro* film will shine all the strengths of this lovely territory, all the humanity of its denizens, all the concerns they have for the future of the Taos Valley. Most importantly, I hope that the movie, and this book will help add to a wider awareness of the need to protect what remains, and to change what isn't working coherently for us now.

For what remains, always, is a fragile beauty that we can ill afford to squander.

ONE

—

On the

—

Brink

—

# of Oceans

—

Mesa road, Picuris Peak.

For the most part, my people come from towns, perched on the edges of two continents, overlooking the Atlantic Ocean. Having the vast seascape available within a stone's throw of their lives is important to their senses of time and place; it helps give them a strong cultural and historical identity. Most of my own life I never lived very far from the sea. Much of the rich tradition giving purpose to my blood is connected with sailing vessels and man-o'-war birds; with Breton fishermen and Salem sea captains; with the terns that wheel above sand dunes on Fire Island.

But for the last eight years I have lived in the shadow of northern New Mexico's high mountains, in a tough, semi-arid valley, surrounded by wide vistas of sagebrush mesa land and bordered on the west by a deep river gorge, a thousand miles from the sound of pounding breakers. I thought at first I would experience a discomfort from being trapped inland, so far from every reinforcement that mere access to beaches and water craft has meant to me. Yet, to my surprise, since I arrived in Taos in 1969 I have never had a longing for the Atlantic shore.

29

Clouds over Pedernal.

Whatever gifts of mood, space and love the ocean once gave me, these southern Rockies have conjured up also. I can stand in my back field, gazing at the nearby peaks, feeling as centered as I ever felt on the threshold of an ocean. I can get my bearings against the silhouette of these Sangre de Cristos as easily as once I could reaffirm a cultural and physical balance against the sound of South Shore waves.

The bulk of these mountains is oceanic. In the place of whales, sharks and porpoises they have mountain lions, elk, and bears. Their currents and reefs are beautiful meadows, talus slopes, thick forests and streams full of trout. Their albatrosses and sea gulls are buzzards, ravens, and golden eagles.

Weather tumbles out of the mountains just as it rolls off the changing sea. Like the sea, these mountains can be dangerous, sudden, inexplicable — they can engulf and kill easily, then roll over and seem as gentle and as compassionate as a summer meadow, and you wonder how ever you could have feared them.

The mysteries and the myths involved with the Atlantic I have known

Lightning near Tres Orejas.

are like the ballads and the superstitions raised by the Sangre de Cristos. And, as does the ocean, these mountains give the people who live in or near them an especially majestic perspective that helps to enlighten their daily struggles, and offers them the chance, if they will take it, to be larger than life.

So I have never felt at all trapped by this inland landscape. In fact, every day I feel the same way I have always felt when living on the brink of oceans.

We went often [for wood], and the hard work felt mighty good. The spectacular drive over was occasionally offset by a dangerous return journey, but the rhythm and mood of the activity made up for everything. That wood gathering facilitated our New York withdrawal, it calmed us a bit, allowing experimentation with other gears to see which new one might help us accelerate into the next stage of existence.

To get to where the Big Jack was leveling and conveniently packaging the forest, we followed Ranchitos Road around the western edge of the valley to Los Córdovas, turned right onto the mesa, dropped into the Rio Grande

31

The old bus full of wood.

Gorge and pushed twenty miles beyond. Nearing Route 285, we turned left onto a raised bed that used to be the narrow-gauge trestle heading for La Servilleta. For the next few miles we zoomed along at a fast clip, straddling deep ruts, praying not to catch a tire and have a blowout or break an axle or flip over. This five-mile suicide run carried us to the desolate country of the Big Jack, where an entire forest was leveled and a dusty silence might be broken only by the shadow of dreamy vultures circling a mile above it all.

Yet that desolation had a tremendous richness given special intensity by our labor. The isolation, the aspects of holocaust, were beautiful. Given the fragile, wild land, all life and weather seemed notoriously special. One day, clumps of brittle roadside grasses swarmed with silky gray caterpillars. Next day, the lifeless area was spooky, church-like, unreal. Unhurriedly, we gathered wood in hot silence, surrounded by surreal weather. In the east over Taos rain lifted off the mountains, a herd of fluffy clouds retreating up and away from pitch-black hills. Between the mountains and the rain clouds, a lovely yellow sky melted into aqua tones, limpid and clear. Directly over our

Typical autumn sky.

heads, a dozen shades of gray merging in a subtle gouache kept shifting with underplayed dramatic effects. A funny thunder, muttering and sighing inarticulately, puttered around in the sky. As the day died, a few big raindrops fell, but no deluge occurred. As night deepened to the east, the air became curiously vibrant: Luke's lemony-white hair glowed as if on fire. To the west gray clouds framed sunny patches of horizon sky: nearby, falling rain was a rouge mist stretching for miles. Every minute jagged lightning flickered down through the gentle smirrh and faint thunder boomed.

Standing in darkness we watched this show. Bunches of purple flowers dotting the desolation were lit up by the electric darkness like underwater neon bouquets. Barely able to see each other, we gathered final armloads of piñon. Only a streak of horizon was visible, like the light shining from under a heavy theater curtain after the houselights have gone out, just before the curtain rises. A radiant streak a hundred miles long, its clean emerald-green sky was broken at intervals by heavy black clouds out of which delicate gauzy strokes of pink rain were falling.

Taos Mountain from the back yard.

Often I wandered aimlessly, a little drugged, not knowing exactly what to do or think or feel, soaking up air, smells, countryside, feeling weather and temperature in my bones, filing scenery and wildlife in a memory bank for my future generations to enjoy. I bought a bicycle, fitting the back with a kiddie seat, and began pedaling along Ranchitos Road in the afternoons. If I was nervous, that slow-motion tripping calmed me down. From time to time I grew so sleepy pedaling aimlessly, that I would close my eyes and drift blindly along the deserted road, the sun hot against my face and shoulders: I listened to the sound of wind, faraway sheep bells, a chattering kingfisher.

For fun I might carry a transistor radio in my basket tuned to the local station, KKIT. I coasted along listening to faint strains of Spanish ranchera music from the afternoon platter show of Judge Norbert Martínez. A midafternoon sunshine pacified the valley. Dogs sprawled in their dusty yards couldn't rouse themselves to charge me snarling. Cattle eyed me with ridiculous bovine stupidity. Only the eyes of horses followed me; they never

Taos Mountain from Ranchitos Road.

turned their heads. I savored the tranquillity, often laughing for joy over my pure and irresponsible inactivities. It was like gliding through cream: my whole body was infused with a low-key near orgasm as I goofily propelled that bicycle along Ranchitos Road.

I had a camera and binoculars. After supper Luke and I pedaled two miles down the road, halting when we saw an old-fashioned hay wagon with slatted sides and soft rubber wheels crossing a field. Two massive white work horses pulled the wagon: they were silhouetted against Taos Mountain, on which vibrant russet sunlight lingered. Later we photographed a horse grazing in darkness, only several highlights visible on its flanks and along its neck. Behind the animal another of those enormous clouds, whose undersides were dissolving, let fall pink cotton-candy rain wisps reaching half-way to the mesa. To the west a black almond-shaped cloud, isolated in an otherwise clear sky, had a fiery magenta rim.

Riding home, I kept up a chatter with Luke, calling his attention to bats, to a little camposanto near a corral in which three mangy buffaloes grunted.

Storm in the back field.

At a favorite overhang, I stopped and looked down on a prairie-dog village of several dozen families. But by then Luke was sound asleep, tilted half out of his kiddie chair, his mouth wide open, his little fists clenched in his groin, snoring loudly.

Almost immediately after unlocking the front door and taking possession, we traveled south to renew acquaintances with Justin Locke, the man whose house I had visited for a week during my first summer out West: instantly, we became fast friends.

Summertime being Justin's season, he was always enthusiastically hoeing, irrigating, fixing his roof, killing ants, pruning, harvesting, caulking, clipping—you name it. And sneezing nonstop, his eyes watering from the wide variety of lovely grasses clinging to his terraced hillsides.

Just sitting on his evening hillside was an adventure. Sheep bells clanked lazily. Magpies and other birds drifted among the cool orchard trees below.

Evening, Pedernal.

White beehives gave character to several fields. Occasionally, a pickup truck chugged along a dirt road crossing the valley, trailing a wake of dust that spread out woozily on either side of the road in slow motion. Sunflowers bloomed: several untended fields looked solidly yellow. In other fields, green alfalfa plants were almost obliterated by a blanket of their own purple flowers.

Walking onto the mesa behind Justin's house, we sat down on rocks among sagebrush plants and juniper trees, buffeted gently by warm evening winds, gazing westward at the usual disgustingly apropos sunset. Overhead a few bats, swallows, and nighthawks did their thing. Travelling southwest toward the Jemez, our eyes always focused on miniature Pedernal, the mesa mountain of Abiquiu, as special in its way as our own hill, important—given its special shape among rounded mountains—distinctly attractive.

I helped Justin irrigate his place. It was like splashing water over a twenty-tiered wedding cake. Channels and little acequias led every which way, looped into this lawn, a garden, fruit trees, gurgling through an intricate system of ditches that zigzagged everywhere, dropping from one terraced level to the

The Pacheco ditch, front yard.

next like an aquatic Slinky—a fabulous, also demented arterial system, managed by a madman.

Justin stabbed his shovel into the earth and presto! the apricot tree by the bedroom had enough to drink for another two weeks. He opened a tiny wooden head gate and a crimson vine—like a beautiful insidious thing from Rappaccini's garden—breathed deeply. If he plunked a rock in the **Y** where a small ditch diverged, water bypassed his cellar door, circled a beehive oven and a tool shed, shot part of its wad in a garden choked with bionic greenery, and plunged downhill to make soggy a cliff of timothy so thick even a snake couldn't slither through it.

Another diversion tumbled water over a rock ledge into thick grass on the narrow open area just before the valley drop-off in front of the house. Stripping naked, we cavorted in the icy waterfall, gasping. Then stood glistening on the edge of the sharp hill, hands on our hips, overlooking the fertile world—overplayed, arrogant, opulent, a scene straight out of a Ken Russell movie or an Ayn Rand novel, Justin all brown beside me, and myself

Taos Mountain from the valley . . .

white as a snowflake against the verdant mood, aspen leaves clattering soundlessly in the background like a trillion deaf-mute bells.

I went into the back field and performed a ritual that often calms me down. From the center of that small patch of brome, I stared at Taos Mountain. It always soothes me, that mountain. It is the most personal geological formation I have ever experienced. . . .

Most of the land from which this special peak rises belongs to the Taos tribe, so I have never hiked that land. And in a way I hope I never will. Right now the unique mass of its powerful but friendly shape is perfect. If I ventured too close its overall beauty might melt into its own trees; its power, for me, might dissolve as it became less than the sum of all its parts.

Always over me or beside me, the mountain inhabits almost every landscape defining my days. If I visit friends at the pueblo, it loses shape, growing top-heavy and elliptical—I am too close. Triangular ridges, outcroppings, and canyons travelling up its slopes admit too real dimensions.

. . . from the mesa . . .

I feel more comfortable when I can drop back, allowing topography to dissolve into flatter planes, becoming part of a single impressive bulk, more of a symbol, I suppose, than a living thing.

Always, the mountain shapes any landscape I am in. Tiny or enormous, it claims the heart of every panorama here, always attracting the eye. From the town dump on the flat mesa land north of Taos, the mountain surges slowly out of a treeless mauve expanse like a powerful, benevolent creature rising from the sea. From my back field the mountain hovers protectively over the tiny Ranchitos community in which I live — a few mud houses, corrals and haystacks, some trailers, and a simple adobe church with a wooden bell

. . . from the gorge.

tower. In town, robbed of a natural foreground, the mountain shrinks, inundated by motel, hotel, gas stations, bank, and restaurant signs. Yet fifteen miles farther south, seen from the rim of the Rio Grande Gorge above a tiny village called Pilar, the mountain resides at the center of a stunning panorama. Taos evening lights twinkle insignificantly at the base of the wide peak like a thin line of phosphorus splashed at the foot of an enormous oceanic wave.

TWO

Cycles of Life

Aspens near Garcia Park.

S tarting in September, in the valley, our eyes rise toward the mountains, waiting for the aspen to launch their melodramatic spectacle. Say what you will about their picture-postcard souls, the aspens make it official. If it is a bland, dry autumn, they take forever to turn. In other years, dampness and early frosts can trigger their excesses prematurely, and the show dies aborning. Occasionally, the foliage never truly ripens: it starts to flare, then suddenly nose-dives into mottled beiges, browns and even blacks. And that robust cliché yellow we love to gawk at never happens.

But oh, when all the elements fall together and great swathes of mountainside blossom with that scintillating radiance! Never mind if it has been versified and adulated to death, each year that the aspens truly turn gold renews our faith and amazement. I nurture no belief in God, but when this

Snoozing near Bernardin Lake.

beautiful death goes down I'm willing to grant to those who do trust in some hallowed diety at least a clever and arrogant magician out there, mischievously and with acute dexterity, amid a swirl of star-bedecked Arabian robes, working his or her overweening, and yet totally captivating sleight of hand.

Nothing can go wrong among the aspens. They remind me of virginity: slim, pure, obnoxiously unblemished. Pristine and serene, they do not dominate, are too pretty to be useful. As fuel, they can't compete with piñon — they die too fast and leave a lot of ash. I consider them above it all, a ruling class — trees without calluses. Could they but speak, their words would descend from those giddy heights on English accents. Don't tell anybody, but I also suspect they are rather stupid.

Bernardin Lake.

Another favorite and easily accessible high-country place is Bernardin Lake. Small and man-made, it used to be a lumber-company wash pond. Then, for a while, Game and Fish stocked it with cutthroats; we used to catch them on little dry flies. But they quit planting trout, I suppose because of winterkill. One autumn I hiked up with my fishing rod, and, instead of trout, I found an empty pond hosting what looked like a demolition derby between a handful of bulldozers.

Evidence that beavers are active in the area is copious — they have made mincemeat of entire sapling forests around the shore . . . yet we have never actually seen a beaver. A reason may be that my kids, Luke and Tania, and their friends always amuse themselves by rolling huge logs down the west-side cliffs into the water, or by peppering the glassy surface for hours with skipping stones. Yet, even when I have been at the lake alone, seated quietly on the bank opposite the mound, I've never seen a beaver.

On the south ridge above the lake, the aspen forest is made up of many young trees, growing very close together. I enjoy resting in that reedy grove,

47

Seventh Latir Lake.

or prowling through it feeling a bit like plankton sifting through a huge whale baleen. Captured among all those slim spears, I experience an excitement of place difficult to explain. Maybe that secretive grove reminds me of childhood hiding places. Perhaps I am touched again by the thrill of a five-year-old's breathless anticipation . . . when I used to crouch among lilac bushes in Montpelier, Vermont, or in evergreen trees behind the house in Wilton, Connecticut, cap pistols cocked, waiting to ambush a playmate, or one of my little brothers.

Tania Nichols among the sunflowers.

S o it begins in the high country, and then moves to a lower elevation, in the shadow of icy mountains.

Warblers appear in the trees, flitting inexhaustibly for a few days, then disappear. One day the siskins arrive, falling out of the north busily atwitter to pluck the sunflowers clean. When I shake the apple trees, hard, glistening fruits bounce painfully off my head. They land in thick swirls of long grass. I hunt them down like Easter eggs, place them on layers of straw in cardboard boxes, and know I'll still be gnawing them in April, wrinkled skins and all.

Grackles at kitchen feeder.

I awaken at 10:00 A.M. The sun is stupendously shining. The frigid air of my yard is spotless. But the eastern hills are vague silhouettes behind a thick haze over town—caused by a thousand wood fires burning. In my kitchen stove I light newspapers and kindling, then dole out grain to the bird-feeders. Instantly, flocks of iridescent black grackles arrive and start posturing belligerently at each other, snapping up tidbits between pufferies. I carry a cup of coffee to the outhouse, and sit with the door open, still groggy. The black cat, Duke, out all night on a hunt, angles up to say howdy. As I pull burrs from his tail, he flops on his back, playfully batting my fingers. Then he hops lightly onto an old sawhorse and settles there, sleepily observing some juncos in the woodpile. Harbingers of cold weather, those gray little birds have only recently materialized.

Horse in a neighbor's field.

I sip my coffee and grin idiotically at the juncos. The orchard and garden area today is host to a flight of black-and-white warblers. Plus a half-dozen western grosbeaks. But the last meadowlark has migrated; the redwing blackbirds will soon be gone. A faint odor of skunk lingers near the outhouse; that, and burning cedar, and a murky redolence from the bogs behind my back field, a mixture of horse dung and mildewed grass.

Duke.

The house is silent. Outside, falling leaves tick against the roof and windows like rain. No wind blows, but leaves are loose on their boughs, and a mysterious, swollen atmospheric pressure pops them loose, as if by magic.

I never rake fallen leaves. Wind sculpts them for me in drifts along garden sheep-fencing, in crevices of the woodpile, against the adobe foundation of the garage, around the roots of lilac bushes south of the kitchen. I can smell

Sparrow hawk in elm leaves.

them through the open window, pungent, decaying, wistful. A light rain commences, instantly catalyzing autumn redolence. Especially the elm leaves carpeting the ground in front of the portal. Mocha, white, and beige, they gleam with an impeccable iridescence, like scales shocked from radiant fishes.

Julian Ledoux.

My friend Julian LeDoux has brought me a cord of piñon. Never have I seen such exquisite fuel. Dry and sharp and professional—it smells like turpentine. The color of this treasure, as I hack away at dusk, is vibrant gray, lucid and clean. Bigotes of furry-green Spanish moss cling to the bark. Each stick I split radiates a gemlike clarity, perfectly textured, a work of art. How can I stoop so low as to *burn* this stuff? Better to sculpt it, place it on pedestals, or just leave it be. So alive is this wood it makes me ache. A soul breathes, not at all inert. Dreamily, I split the tough chunks, feeling happy and sexy.

September grazing, Tres Orejas.

I sometimes wonder how this spare, bony plateau became so hallowed. It has to do, I suppose, with the lack of clutter. Here, my imagination is free to take off because there are not impeding structures. I crave the wild silence it offers, the lack of contact with civilized artifacts, the aloneness I am bequeathed as I wander across the becalmed sagebrush expanse. And I am awed by the reduction of detail in a way that I could never be awed by the cathedral at Chartres, the Taj Mahal, or an Apple computer.

Parking the truck, I slip on my camera pack, squeeze the tripod under one arm, and start walking. I smell the August sagebrush. Dry ring muhly "muffins" are everywhere. It has not rained for months, and dirt as soft as powdered silk puffs up a little at each step. The frayed half-moon-shaped musical notes of dead grama grass tremble delicately. The sky is glaring, hot, boring.

Hairy golden asters, Sangre de Cristo Mountains.

My favorite area of the mesa features a small stock pond near an old sheep corral. The pond has been dry all summer; the sheep corral has been deserted since June. In fact, only in springtime do sheep inhabit this territory. Lambing is done at the corrals, a half-mile south of the stock pond; castration and shearing follow. Driving by at dusk, I've seen an old Airstream trailer at the camp, several men around a cookfire, a battered pickup, and a few hundred animals. It's a dream from a hundred years ago; a gentle and solid valentine from the past.

Rain puddle near stock pond.

Slowly—on a withered August afternoon—I turn, completing a circle, grateful for the emptiness that soothes my agitated soul. Though their majesty always thrills me, the mountains fifteen miles away keep their distance. They never loom overhead, they cast no shadows across this lean space. I am granted all the room in the world for breathing.

Wordsworth wasn't kidding when he wrote: "How gracious, how benign, is Solitude." The French writer St. Exupery had a letch for the loneliness of

Ring muhly.

the small airplanes he piloted across African deserts. And he nurtured an understanding of simplicity. "In anything at all," he once wrote, "perfection is finally attained not when there is no longer anything to add, but when there is no longer anything to take away, when a body has been stripped down to its nakedness."

The patient and benign mesa is not exactly naked, but it is as stripped down and as clean a landscape as I know.

Storm over Tres Orejas.

And now the twilight air grows so still that is seems not to exist. When I walk, the atmosphere offers no resistance. Made almost dizzy by the seductive passivity, I find myself glancing around for evidence of a single invisible current. I stop, then inhale and hold it. The loudest sounds are cataracts of blood roaring through my veins and arteries, the thump of my heart pumping, and some faint, sticky clicks as I wet my lips.

Such quiet air is almost inconceivable. A world so completely halted seems to be an artificial creation of aesthetics rather than a natural phenomenon. It is environment without qualms, sagebrush etched against itself as if into layers of fossilized stone.

Dry grasses throb with faint, argentine luminescence: a slim crescent moon hangs in a clear mauve patch of sky directly above. Everything idle seems to be growing incredibly animated, almost explosively imbued with energy that will erupt when the slightest breeze bearing a raindrop awakens the world.

Road to the sheep corral.

Light is changing, dying, dissolving—but oh, what passionate death throes! I recall childhood days on evening beaches when phosphorus sparks tumbled in sea foam lapping against the sand. It seems a residue of that same fluorescence lingers on the branches, pebbles, and bones around me. Dancing surreal light is achingly intense, and I can smell the rain invisibly swelling around me.

Then the air flares up with a glow transforming this dark moment into such vivid creation that instinctively I cast about for a band of angels, or at least the shimmering outline of a distant saint.

Stock pond after a rain.

You pull the string on a folded-up Chinese paper flower and it pops into being, replete with many serene oriental colors—so the mesa sprouts alive just seconds after the rain and hustles full-tilt toward its own brand of muted glory.

Grasses rise in delicate profusion. Sagebrush grows bushier, adopting a pastel-blue shine. Dry branches of rabbitbrush flush verdant and produce bright yellow flowers. Wild milkweed plants pop up in Coyote Gulch and blossom pinkly; monarch butterflies arrive and lay eggs which spawn caterpillars. Overnight, round ring muhly discs become fluffy halos which soon cover portions of the mesa with a gauze that resembles platters of mist or clumps of soft fur.

October sunset.

Hours after the water is impounded [in the stock pond], mosquitoes and other bugs are running rampant. I begin to see the splash rings of insects being born. It isn't long before green darning needles zip over the muddy pond, chased by aggressive blue and gray dragonflies. Tiny things grab each other, kick and fuss, chew and dismember, eat, digest, and defecate, and then look around hungrily to see if there's anybody they missed: life, elucidated by unending holocaust; the natural world as total war!

However this bucolic slaughterhouse is perceived, on the mesa the spadefoot toads are the first real gauge of the stock pond's awakening. I've read that these small toads spend most of their lives dormant underground: books suggest that the toads sleep for months, "perhaps years" at a time. I have never seen a mature spadefoot, in daylight, on the mesa.

Spadefoot tadpoles.

Yet soon as the stock pond holds water, great hordes of the nocturnal toadlets appear. For a night or two, these mysterious creatures raise a ruckus, bleating at each other stridently as they hop about in a delirious mating ritual I have never witnessed. Since the toads are programmed to reproduce in shallow rain puddles which often last but a week or two, they waste little time in courtship subtleties. It rains, there's water — a mass orgy takes place. Fertilized eggs are cached in the water. And the adult toads vanish, presumably tunneling (backwards) into oblivion, there to await another propitious deluge one year hence.

Collared lizard.

Spadefoot eggs hatch immediately, and the results — a Cecil B. DeMille production of tadpoles — transforms itself from aquatic bumblers to air-breathing adults in a similarly vertiginous time period. *The Guinness Book of World Records* doesn't list the Fastest Spadefoot Conversion in History, but in his work *The Desert Year,* Joseph Wood Krutch tells of a tadpole that completed its metamorphosis from water creature to desert tadpole in eleven days.

Considering that most normal frog tadpoles need from three months to two years to evolve into land-based creatures, the spadefoot dispatch is nothing short of mercurial.

Sheep moths.

One day the pond is quiet; next day thousands of tadpoles are wiggling in the shallow water, feeding voraciously on algae, on mosquito larvae, and (of course) on each other. If I fell in, no doubt these miniature piranha fish would dismember me in seconds. Great bands of tadpoles bob and thrash against the surface, eating insects and gulping air. So many of them simultaneously nibble the atmosphere, that when I hold still I can hear their mouths making a sound like burbling foam on a big head of beer. Dipping cupped hands anywhere into the shallow pond, I can withdraw dozens of squirming polliwogs. . . .

Twilight stock pond.

Yet how quickly the season dwindles! By mid–September most fat and sassy tadpoles have shed their tails and begun migrating from the water. For a week it's difficult to avoid squashing mini-toads underfoot. Still, the puddle teems with polliwogs, and I suspect they'll be in residence all autumn.

Yet a day arrives when an eerie stillness greets me at the stock pond. Amazingly, the tadpoles are *gone*. Oh, a stray polliwog probes stubby aquatic plants near shore, but that's all; and three dehydrated tadpole bodies lie in the muck, skins wrinkled and flat, emptied of flesh and fluids. As for the rest of their minions—? Cleared out, disappeared, kaput. A massive exodus

December snowstorm.

onto dry land occurred at night while I was elsewhere. For a special moment the pond must have seemed as crazy as a Tokyo subway emptying at rush hour; surely moonlight spotlighted all those slippery, coin-sized amphibians as they emerged en mass in toadlet pandemonium.

Whatever else happened, the spadefoots received their mysterious nod from the universe, bailed out of their aquatic prison, and, with nary a fare-thee-well in my direction, they vanished off the face of the earth.

Winter thaw.

A moment ago the mesa was flourishing. Now it is withered again . . . or all gone underground.

Winter keeps approaching; the landscape is increasingly stark. Nearly finished are the bird migrations. Rain quits falling altogether. Bleak yet soft are the shortening days. Sunshine drapes thinly over impervious sage. Rocks stay cold all day.

Frozen stock pond.

A mere puddle remains where once stood the teeming stock pond. A deserted air frames the mood; animals tunnel still deeper. Prairie dogs no longer stand noisy watch on the rims of their hills. Ants have gone dormant beneath their pebble cones. I cease being alert for rattlesnakes.

On evenings for a week a lone nighthawk quarters the air over the stock pond, hunting penultimate insects. Then the discouraged bird gives up, travels south. A single bat feeds over the small reservoir in which the evening star is reflected—pickings must be slim.

Lone hawk at dusk.

A serious stillness overtakes the plateau. Now is the time of bones and feathers, of small talismans left behind—the residue of all the mesa's hasty aliveness.

I notice a white reflection deep in the crevice between two boulders. Reaching down, I grasp a small jackrabbit skull. For a while I inspect the brittle structure, fascinated by the wingèd shape of eye sockets, by the tiny teeth, by the intricate webbings of bone and the detailed zig-zagging cracks across the paper thin cranium. I could easily get lost in the study of elfin skulls. The craftmanship in Lilliputian jawbones and miniature teeth seems so far beyond any artistic expression humans could invent. When I choose

Dead magpie.

to look closely at anything — a skull, a dried flower, a snakeskin — its perfect complexity tunnels into my brain. The intricate symmetry of a rabbit skull can hold its own with the fantastic vaulted knaves of medieval cathedrals.

Coyote skull.

In several gullies are rib bones, slim and curved, quicksilver graceful, like wands fallen from the hands of invisible curanderas floating overhead. I sail one through the air, a lightweight boomerang, a skeletal feather. The elegant cleanliness of its lines is fluent and alluring. I run my finger along the chaste, curving length—so harmonious and classic.

"If we could polish our souls with bones, what a powerful simplicity might light up the world!"

Road to the stock pond.

Across the moon I wander, pausing to take photographs. At intervals I halt, responding to the environment by staying quiet, by listening to the silence, by letting myself relax. For miles no tracks tell stories in the unblemished mantle. Have all the small hibernators been suffocated already? I expected fresh holes where rabbits and kangaroo rats had tunneled out. Yet all I come across, finally, is a single raven-sized wing print in the powder.

January wind drifts.

All snowdunes slant gracefully in a northeasterly direction. The wind must have whistled last night. I'm glad it's shut down now. My eyes soon hurt from squinting.

I pass black and brown cows mournfully standing around, wondering: what next? Steam boils out of their nostrils. Mountains are bleached from top to bottom, and their whiteness merges with the snowy mesa, and the snowcover travels west until it fades into the cerulean blue atmosphere. . . .

Freezing cattle.

Right now this arctic mood belongs solely to me. I own the mountains; the sky begins expanding an inch above my shoulders. The solitude creates a rapture inside me.

Creak, creak, my boots advance. Until, for the last time, I halt, turning a circle, gazing all around. I don't want to lose it, I suppress feelings of loss. Perhaps I can't ever reproduce the satisfaction of this moment; maybe I'll never again have such reverence for life. It doesn't matter. The most precious gifts often dissolve off my fingertips within a moment of their triumphs. . . .

The stock pond disappears.

We are touched by magic wands. For just a fraction of our day life is perfect, and we are absolutely happy and in harmony with the earth. The feeling passes much too quickly. But the memory—and the anticipation of other miracles—sustains us in the battle indefinitely.

THREE

The People . . .
Yes

Andrés and Jeannette Martínez.

There is still a balance in the Taos Valley. In 1981, a majority of the population remains Spanish-speaking, although census figures suggest that within a decade Anglos may outnumber Chicanos. Certainly, a vast majority of the valley's businesses are owned by relative newcomers, who effectively control the economy. But there are still some land-based old-timers, their children, and a few concerned newcomers struggling to keep the more important traditions intact.

One such person is my longtime friend, Andrés Martínez. Most deeply, Andrés believes in the land. He has worked hard to protect it, and to preserve sensibilities that venerate it. The basis upon which his life and vitality is founded is the understanding that when you kill the land, you destroy the human soul.

Not long ago, Andrés said he wanted to climb Tres Orejas, the odd mountain that rises from the sagebrush plain west of town, on the other side of the gorge. Although just turned eighty, he had never climbed that three-eared cerro, a physical and spiritual reference point throughout his life. As

Sheep south of Tres Orejas.

a young boy, during the first decade of the twentieth century, he had herded sheep on the plain surrounding the isolated hill. But he had always been too busy to climb it.

Then he left Taos for many years, going to school, teaching, traveling, starting a family, holding down different jobs. For a while, with his first wife, Dorothy, Andrés ran a Navajo trading post in Atarque, New Mexico . . . and that is one of his favorite places, though it is all gone now. . . . A man named Dent, who owned a castle near the Garden of the Gods in Colorado, hired my friend. Later, he wanted to set Andrés up with some cattle over in the Texas panhandle. But Dorothy exclaimed, "Oh my God, not the panhandle! All those *winds!*"

So instead, one day after World War II, Andrés and Dorothy blew back into Taos, and launched a small dairy farm in that section of the valley known as Talpa. From the top of his outbuildings, and from his haystacks, Andrés could gaze across the plain to that distant three-pronged peak, in whose

shadow he had spent many a boyhood day, tending Gregorio Mondragón's sheep.

Still, he never got over there to climb it. Andrés and Dorothy struggled to keep afloat in the dairy business, but eventually lost out to corporate dairies commandeering the Taos market. Finally, they retired and moved to a trailer in Cañon, closer to town. Then Dorothy died, and Andrés lived alone for a while, farming land for his church, irrigating two of his own acres, gathering wood each autumn, drying fruits and vegetables, making chicos of white corn, and in general keeping busy and keeping fit.

In his late seventies, Andrés drove off to California to visit an old family friend, recently widowed. And he returned to Taos shortly thereafter with a new wife, Jeannette, and a desire to climb Tres Orejas while still in the pink of condition.

I said, "Sure, why not?" After all, I had been in the valley ten years already, yet I had never climbed that mountain myself.

Andrés atop Tres Orejas.

Tres Orejas sits in the middle of an ocean, a unique and fascinating silhouette. As we started up, Andrés deserted his English and began speaking Spanish. We moved easily through juniper and piñon forest. Fresh deer tracks crisscrossed the loose, dusty earth: flickers disappeared into the trees. We paused and gathered piñon nuts, shelling them between our teeth, gladly tasting the meat already roasted by weeks under a hot sun.

Birds sang, unleashing a crescendo of incongruous warbled notes. Beneath a relentless sky the landscape seemed arid and desolate and lonely, yet a virtual orchestra of birds—I guessed sage thrashers or Townsend's solitaires—made it seem we had somehow stumbled into a fertile and dripping wet English country garden!

We proceeded through the lyrical racket. Large black-and-orange wasps floated on the warm currents. Limestone rocks were scattered across the slopes. In former times, explained my friend, people extracted the lime for cooking uses—in posole, in their beans.

"You had to use everything in those days." So saying, Andrés plucked

Antique hay rake on the mesa.

a herb that he calls chimaja: "It's good for stomachaches."

It took forty-five minutes to reach the shadow of the southeast summit. A rock cone rose abruptly, uncomfortably steep on the south side. So we swung around to the north and Andrés started ahead of me. A wren on a nearby rock dipped nervously, then disappeared into a little cave. In a few moments, we reached the top and stood with our hands on our hips, panting and exhilarated. On boulders framed by yellow flowering rabbitbrush lay deposits of weathered deer droppings.

Andrés pointed to a small wooden structure just beyond the eastern foothills of Tres Orejas: "Those corrals belong to Delfino Valerio." A half-mile to the south an abandoned house was surrounded by dead trees. "That's the Graves place," he said. "But nobody lives there anymore."

Miles farther south we could see the five or six buildings comprising the mighty township of Carson, on Route 96. Other than that, very little broke up the beautiful monotony. A tiny weathered ruin, a couple of isolated adobes—like small boats on the otherwise deserted and becalmed sea.

Old boundary cairn.

Dreamily, my friend speaks. He remembers the sheep camps from seventy years ago, and where they were stationed. On that hummock, the Martínezes; over by that arroyo, the Mondragóns. In the old days, all the land below was richer with native grasses; and the sagebrush was twice as tall. The sheep could survive easily in the snow, they had more protection.

Ghosts take flight off the tip of his Spanish tongue. They float into the dusty mauve landscape, inessential shadows. Sheepherders, homesteaders, old pals, fellow children who grew up, left Taos, disappeared into history. Others remained in the valley, hanging on to their sheep, clerking in grocery stores, teaching school—outstanding citizens and goofy outlaws . . . all gone . . . *difuntos* . . . dust.

At the turn of the century, says Andrés, you could ride out and make a camp anywhere and nobody came to ask for a permit, heckle, read riot acts. Hardly any fences enclosed the territory in those days. Some men drove their herds overland as far west as Navajo country. Nothing impeded their

Autumn Rio Grande at Pilar.

progress between here and the horizon — no barbwire, no cities, no private property.

Finally, Andrés sucks in a breath and says thoughtfully: "This is a glorious day for me. I always wanted to do this before I died. I thank God for letting me live long enough to have this experience."

Charley Reynolds has been fishing the Taos County section of the Rio Grande for thirty-three years.

Arbiter and overlord of my discovery of the Rio Grande, Charley is not exactly your average sort of trout fisherman. In fact, Charley often looks like a Bowery bum when he goes fishing. His pants drag halfway down to his ankles. His hat usually resembles something Tom Mix bequeathed to Andy Devine, who then willed it to Slim Pickens. And although Charley is over six feet tall, he simpers along in old army boots, limping and groaning from ancient injuries at each agonized step, so that you wonder how the man can successfully trek in and out of the gorge, let alone pursue trout with the finesse

87

Charley Reynolds, Lobo, and Big Red.

and expertise such stalking requires.

The man's accidents are legendary, and bear some cataloguing here, if only because a commitment to the Rio Grande seems to inflict all anglers with a most puzzling maladroitness on and off the river: Charley is merely one textbook example of the affliction.

I am writing this section in April 1981. Last week I fished with Charley down on the Red River. During our brief outing, Charley fell in the river twice and smashed the face and crystal off his watch. Next day, he traded a painting for a neighbor's motorcycle. Piloting the bike out her driveway, he lost control and plowed through a barbwire fence. Indomitable (and unshakable), he pushed the Honda onto the road and traveled almost to his own front door before dumping the machine again, this time in his own driveway. When I saw him in a supermarket next morning, he regaled me with tales of his moto misfortunes, said, "Yessir, hell ain't far away when you're on the brink of eternity," and generously offered to take me out for a spin on his new deathmobile.

Doug Terry on the Rio Grande.

I have no idea how Charley survives such misfortune. And yet he appears to be relatively healthy. To be sure, as I've mentioned, he limps, the result of an ankle broken on April Fools' Day in the gorge five years ago. But his hands are the only dead giveaway. Big, strong, and blunt, they are also usually quite mangled, callused, bruised, and stained with leatherworking dyes. Several black-and-blue fingernails sport small round holes where Charley has relieved the pressure of blood blisters by drilling red-hot paper clips through the nail—one of life's more painful remedies.

Charley has always told me that he ain't much on doctors.

Or mechanics. Witness his 1973 red Dodge truck called Big Red (RIP). A sign on the driverside door said IT TAKES LEAD BALLS TO SHOOT MUZZLE-LOADERS. Big Red feared no terrain. The first few times I passengered to the gorge rim in Big Red, I felt like the inhabitant of a Sherman tank racing through pitfalls at El Alamein. Charley definitely liked Big Red to get him places *toot sweet*. Whenever we parked, he opened the hood and yanked sage branches out of the fanbelt. Then he shoved a large saucepan

Mike Kimmel.

under Big Red to catch combustible fluids leaking from the truck's rock-dented gas tank, so on our return we could pour gas back into the truck, and make it home.

Big Red is with us no more, even though at this writing he resides in Charley's driveway, awaiting a sucker with three hundred dollars to tow him away.

Charley, however, remains hearty and hale as he heads into the gorge looking like a cross between Wyatt Earp and Pappy Yokum. A self-admitted "bear cub in boxing gloves" who can swing a fly rod as well as Minnesota Fats handles a pool cue, Charley is, quite simply, one of New Mexico's premier precision sporting machines, a gallivanting conglomeration of guts, arrogance, instinct, and talent that can outfish, outhunt, outexplore, and outtalk anybody.

I called Mike Kimmel, a writer friend in Philadelphia, and begged him to fly out for three weeks of gorge exploring, trout fishing, and Wild Turkey 101.

Kimmel snapping for browns on a little river.

Mike and I go way back. Guatemala in 1964, shortly after a state of siege, is where we met. Mike was at work in a small town for the American Friends. He is about five feet, four inches tall, and a very macho fellow in his black T-shirts, pegged dungarees, and black Wellingtons with Cuban heels. Mike comes on in a manner that might be described as "strong." Five minutes after we met he claimed he was the only guy ever number one in his major at Temple who could also run fifty balls shooting straight pool. Assessing him with a jaundiced eye, I figured he was too loud to be authentic, and accepted the challenge. Me, whose sporting career consisted of maybe ten games in a Utica pool hall and three viewings of *The Hustler.* Mike snapped "I'll even spot you twenty-five balls." I replied, "Fuck you, I'll take 'em!" He won the toss and broke the rack. Ten minutes later he flubbed a ball at the end of his second rack, and I had a chance to play. I sank one ball, then scratched. I lost the match 50 to 26, and took a closer look at Mike Kimmel.

Andrés Martínez gave me the Taos Valley, much of its history and water lore, the western mesa, and the old sheep camps in the shadow of the Tres

Mike Kimmel on the Little Rio Grande.

Orejas. Charley Reynolds offered the Rio Grande and the difficult prehistoric gorge through which it travels. Years earlier, Mike Kimmel opened up something different. He gave me city streets and stickball mythologies, Palestra chaos and corner boys in a cappella reveries. He offered the rhythm of ghetto and city cultures on an energetic platter, and irrevocably altered the cadences—in my life and my work—by transmitting unashamedly a volatile, positive, proud, and argumentative energy that has vastly enriched my life. A fine writer himself, he took seriously my art from the start . . . and in a fierce way that has invariably bolstered me during hard times.

Among other accomplishments, Mike is a *serious* fisherman. In the old days, when not carting trays in the Catskills, he was working party boats. Even today he'll take off on a weekend, drive to the South Jersey shore, rent a rowboat, and drift around catching flounders, just to be able to say he's "gone fishin." Or on a Saturday morning he might hike over to the Schuylkill—the Schuylkill, for crissakes!—and catch a catfish or a bass.

Years ago, in the early seventies, when Mike first visited New Mexico,

Brown trout.

I stuck a fly rod in his hands, which had never held a fly rod, and packed him off to the minuscule Rio Chiquito, wherein mighty spooky little brown trout flourished. I figured: Now I punish Mike for that skunking in Guatemala. And, as he tripped over a vine, caught his fly on a juniper, and spooked half a mile of river, I chortled. At which point he raised his eyebrows, removed his pipe, and gestured emphatically with it as his upper lip curled into a fat sneer. Jaw jutted, he said, "Oh, no, Nichols, wait a minute, not me—I ain't another one of your turkeys, I'll figure it out, you son of a bitch, then I'll mop the river with your ass!"

Later (rather than sooner), but still later (rather than never), he made good his vow. It took him half a season, though, and it is probably the first time in New Mexico history that any significant numbers of trout have fallen to an angler wearing a cobra-shaped pinkie ring.

That was a season, then—the autumn of 1979. Thanks to Charley Reynolds, Mike and I learned the Rio Grande is indeed a spectacular

Rainbow and brown.

and movable feast whose waters positively teem with silvery fish . . . and, what's more, you can catch 'em.

We caught them. And we lost them. I still have dreams of all the lunkers I hooked that year; big rainbows tear upwards toward the sky like miniature tarpon, dancing across the ripples on their tails in great sprays of sun-drenched agua. Sometimes they dive to the bottom under heavy surging water, shake their heads twice, and are gone. On other occasions they hit my fly so hard and voraciously there's nothing but an abrupt *doink!* as leader and fly part company, and some monster heads downriver with the little barb stuck in its cruel-looking underslung jaw.

I soon started using a leader rigged with a tail fly and two droppers, and once hooked a twelve-inch trout and an eighteen-incher on the same cast. Gunshot-sudden, the bigger fish bellied over two feet above the river and snapped the line—but I landed the twelve-incher.

North on the river, between Bear Crossing and Ox Trail, Mike struck something that felt like a log. He tried to unsnag his fly with a tug, and up

Snowstorm on the Rio Grande.

came the biggest trout he'd ever seen, perhaps in the five-pound class. Moving deliberately, the fish gave one smooth dolphinesque leap, spit out the hook, and reentered the water without a splash.

Mike was sitting on a rock, blue in the face, smoking his pipe and trying to regain his composure, when Charley approached and said, "Well, would you rather a not of hooked it?" Mike almost brained him with a rock.

I love it. Every last fatal, traumatic, and bewitching moment of my time on the Rio Grande. On each new trip, when I arrive at the rim and gaze down, it is like reaching the other side of a magic mountain and viewing a scene toward which my imagination has strained for ages. No two days are alike. Always, I expect some rare treasure to be revealed: of weather, mood, the animal kingdom.

My passion for it, I think, makes the river dangerous. My lust to cover ground, my intense fishing concentration, my fanatical need to push on around the next corner, even at the cost of retreating back two miles across boulders

95

Night on the Rio Grande.

in impenetrable darkness, changes the nature of the experience—also its consequences. I adore the risk of staying keyed-up and perfectly balanced while rushing through the night, weighed down by my camera pack and a gunnysack full of lunkers, the whole universe captured tensely in the flickering beam of a flashlight across the cruel labyrinth of giant stones. Hard work, sure, but I feel terribly loose and rhythmic and cocky among the rocks. Not since college days have I reveled in a similar euphoria and confidence. Every muscle strains to react correctly, yet I am permeated by a languorous wild joy. Blind to my surroundings, I know exactly where I stand.

I am with Doug Terry in November. The sky is absolutely unblemished, cobalt blue, almost phony, an acrylic pretension by some meticulous guru of pop art. Sunshine oozes like syrup over warm boulders. The river is as clear as glycerin.

A hundred yards above Brown Trout Alley, I say, "Whoa, walk quietly, let's sneak up and see if the monster is feeding."

The author, dressed sloppy, with a small lunker (18").

The author, dressed fancy, with a small lunker (19").

Hunched over, we approach cautiously. In midstream is a large boulder. Twice before I have noticed a huge, torpedo-shaped shadow in front of the rock, two feet below the surface, placidly sucking in tidbits, a wild and wily brown in at least the ten-pound range. A dozen different artificial offerings dropped delicately before its toro-sized nostrils have never produced a nibble. We are dealing, here, with a survivor.

We creep within range and sure enough, the torpedo is up and exposed, quietly noshing. Nearby, several smaller obsequious fish are munching on waterborn delicacies. A three-pound eighteen-incher repeatedly dimples for tiny yellow insects, an emaciated sardine compared to the *capo di tutti capo* beneath it. A few one-pound minnows are merely finning lazily, deferring to their elders.

But as we try to sneak closer, they evaporate. Only the monster retreats slowly, backing into the rock shadows where no doubt it has lived for many a season.

Isabel and Evelyn.

A few of them remain, then, murderous and untouchable in the blue depth of certain pools, golems of the Rio Grande, evolved beyond vulnerability . . . the legends that keep us going.

On all the human levels that count, Isabel Vigil and her daughter, Evelyn Mares, are two very special people. Somehow, they have endured more adversity than I could hope to combat in a dozen lifetimes. And their lives, their energies are a real inspiration to me.

Isabel is like a character from *The Grapes of Wrath* or *The People, Yes.* In her life is the poetry and hardship contained within the universal human spirit. Summing up that spirit, as we did recently when Isabel's husband finally died after a ten-year illness, you sure can't laugh off her capacity to take it.

Cowboy Joe Vigil was Isabel's second husband and her true love: he suffered an incapacitating stroke in 1970. Thereafter, he was an invalid. For a decade, Isabel and her daughter Evelyn cared for Joe, a legendary man in the Taos Valley who would not die. But at long last, in the summer of 1980,

Pasque flowers.

he reentered the hospital for the umpteenth time, and the doctors figured by then he was probably tired enough to let go.

Isabel's original name was Lorrita Elizabeth Sanks, and she hated it. Soon as she could do it legally, she had it changed to Isabel Rita Stanhope. "That was after a silent-movie star of those days, her name was Isabel Stanhope. As I remember, she was mostly in jungle pictures. . . ."

Because her dad had difficulty maintaining a family, Isabel grew up in and out of orphanages, in Nebraska and Montana.

In the middle of the Depression, age sixteen, Isabel walked away from the orphanage and hitchhiked south to Idaho Falls. She had nothing to her name except the dress on her back and a Bible. Her shoes had come apart— the soles flopped noisily, so she found baling cord in a field and tied them together. Though all alone on the road for several days, nothing bad happened. She ate berries and slept under the stars. And remembers that trip as one of the most wonderful and liberated moments of her life. . . .

99

Tanya Mares and Tania Nichols.

Not long after, she met a fellow and got married: his name was Mares. Eventually, they settled in Gallup, New Mexico. Isabel started bearing children, and the hard times came in droves. She miscarried twice; two other babies died. For one of them, a girl, her husband wouldn't let her go to the hospital. "He got a Mexican woman to come in. She gave me warm water with pepper in it. I kept vomiting. I had been hemorrhaging off and on for nine months, because, as it turned out later, I had a couple of tumors in there. Finally, the baby came. But something was wrong. And that man didn't know what to do with it. I remember that she had blue eyes, because her eyes were open. But she expired right there in my husband's arms. Her little arms shot out straight when she died. . . ."

The marriage was rough, and Isabel worked hard, trying to raise five kids and hold down a job to keep the rent paid. When the kids matured a little, they about ran her into an early grave.

"They would go out and steal all kinds of stuff from the stores in Gallup. Bob and Tom, that is — but not Larry. Larry was always sick; he had Bright's

disease, so he never went out and did anything. But he was the brains behind a lot of the operations. If the rest of the kids wouldn't split the take with him, he'd threaten to squeal on them — so they always gave him a dollar, or something. . . ."

Finally, it looked like curtains for the Mares teenagers. The family was disintegrating. The authorities planned to ship Tom and Bob off to the Springer Boys' School. In the end, on just two weeks' notice, Isabel packed up the family and fled Gallup, bringing everybody to Taos, the only way to save her boys from reform school. . . .

In Taos, Isabel's luck changed. Desperate for work, she hired on with Cowboy Joe Vigil to be chief cook and bottle washer for him and seven men helping with the haying on his Ranchitos ranch. The job was supposed to last for five days. But Joe, who at the time was a footloose bachelor between marriages, kept her on for twenty-five years. They fell in love, and their first fifteen years were the halcyon days of Isabel's life.

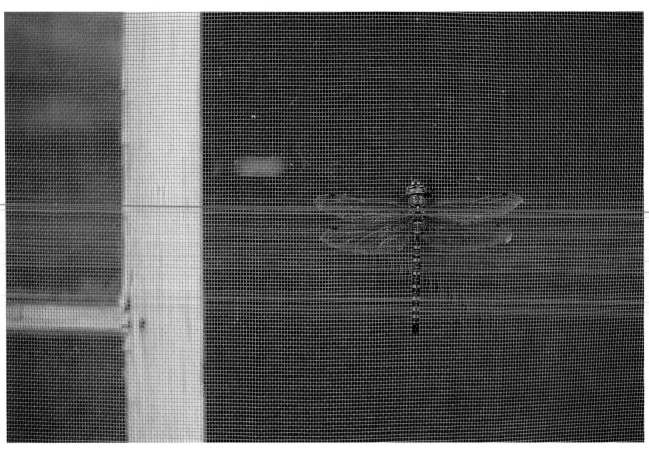
Blue darner dragonfly.

"When he was younger and on the rodeo circuit, he used to go to the bawdy houses up in Wyoming," Isabel told me. "He had a different woman every night. . . ." He had not lived a protected life in other ways, either. Most of his teeth and all of his bones had been broken rodeoing. He had lost the little finger on one hand roping a calf—the hemp just formed a loop, snapped tight, and chopped it off. "And I never could find that finger down in all that dust," Joe told his wife.

Isabel and Joe were a team; on the Ranchitos place, and outside it. The ranch had thirty-two acres of vega land, wide pastures stretching back to the Taos mesa. Through the meadows ditches ran. Little springs beneath the surface made some areas swampy. Hundreds of killdeer populated the fields; flights of wild geese and ducks were always landing. They ran cattle back there, and horses, and a few sheep.

It was a full-time job, caring for the land. But Isabel's recollections are happy. Seems like everybody had a fair share of fun.

The Pueblo River.

Music was a part of their lives. Joe played accordion, piano, harmonica, Jew's harp. He worked hard and played hard, too. He liked his liquor, though it never made him mean.

Stories of Joe's drunks, like stories of the man himself, are legendary. As soon as she heard him arrive home making a commotion that indicated he was in his cups, Isabel would hide, often in the same bed with Evelyn. His accordion to his chest, Joe would creep through the dark house calling, "Honey, where arrrrre you?" And when he found her, he would strike up his favorite Spanish song on the squeeze-box: "Tu y las nubes me traen muy loco. . . ." You and the clouds are driving me crazy!

"And what could I do?" Isabel sighed, chuckling. "I just melted with love. Honestly, that man. . . ."

Now came the hard times. Everybody except Larry, who was increasingly incapacitated by his illness, entered the Army. Evelyn included. They dispersed to army bases in the States, or overseas. Evelyn was the first to come

Horse and colt.

home . . . in shock because her fiancé had just been killed in a California car accident.

In 1970 the stroke felled Cowboy Joe; and of a sudden he was helpless, totally dependent on Isabel.

Then Bob died; he was shot to death in California when he surprised a burglar in his home.

Around that time Danny returned from Vietnam, burned out, on drugs, confused, and floundering. "He was on all kinds of dope," Isabel said, "and we couldn't get him off it."

Danny suffered, and trundled in and out of hospitals. He was scared. Shortly before he died in 1973, Isabel traveled with her son in the ambulance on his final journey. The attendant asked her to hold Danny's kicking feet so they wouldn't be bruised. Tenderly, she held down her son's feet during that drive to the hospital . . . and then Danny too was gone, still in his twenties.

Autumn cottonwood.

Increasingly, Larry grew more helpless. His kidneys deteriorated. For a spell he lived away from home, but eventually—enfeebled and failing—he had to return. Numbed by medications, he became an invalid. Evelyn had worked in Denver for a while; now she returned with a daughter named Tanya, and settled in to help her mom care for her stepfather and her brother.

They rented out the back pastures to earn a little cash; burned off the front field and repaired all the animal pens. Selling peacock feathers earned a few dollars; chicken eggs brought in harder cash. They robbed Peter to pay Paul, managed to get Medicaid and welfare payments, bought clothes at church rummage sales, sold turkeys and geese and goats, gathered apples, put up heaps of their own garden vegetables, and tried to repair the house, which was slowly crumbling—just Evelyn and Isabel, the two invalids, and a little child. Tom had married and was living outside Denver.

Then, in 1977, Larry gave up his prolonged struggle with Bright's disease, and died.

Bottom of dry stock pond after a snowstorm.

That left just Isabel and Evelyn on the ranch, taking care of Cowboy Joe. Within a decade, almost the entire family had been leveled prematurely.

When I first met them not long after Larry's death, I never would have guessed that so much hardship had badgered their lives. Their house seemed like a wonderful hobo castle, cluttered with a billion knicknacks and photos, children's paintings, aquariums, green plants, and rich smells from the kitchen. Outdoors they had playhouses for kids, dozens of flower planters full of snoozing kittens, a regular army of Chihuahua-sized dogs yipping about, big malamutes and gorgeous puppies in pens, herds of geese racing down the driveway to splash in the irrigation ditches. Goats cavorted in old jerry-rigged corrals, a horse and her colt meandered about. Lilacs bloomed, other flowers blossomed, bees congregated at hives by the little trout pond.

Yet their poverty, the struggle to hang on to their place and keep it vital, has been real taxing.

Sunset from the back yard.

"I'm pooped," Evelyn murmured on a sunny Saturday last year. "I'm so tired of never having any money. Of always reaching into my pocket, and finding a dollar—one lousy dollar—and knowing that it's supposed to last for fifteen days...."

Still, they never moped for long. Forever on the edge, they bitched and laughed, cared for Cowboy Joe, harvested apples and collected eggs, helped Melissa foal a blue-eyed colt called Pickles, worried about the thistles threatening valuable pastureland, plucked destructive foxtail by hand from the fields, cooked up hummingbird syrup for their feeders, and in general worked themselves half to death maintaining a healthy quality of life.

At the heart of their lives lay the quiet heavy bulk of Cowboy Joe, whom they cared for, loved dearly, and knew one day would die. "He wants to leave me now," Isabel used to say. "I can tell he's real tired. But I don't want him to go yet. I love him so much. I can't let him get away...."

107

Pacomio Mondragón and Andrés Martínez.

No matter. During the first week of July, in 1980, Cowboy Joe Vigil, age eighty-three, finally died. Isabel said, "We sat with him while he took his final gasps. I felt so bad, because there was no way I could help him. One nurse even gave him mouth-to-mouth resuscitation. But nothing worked. He was so tired, and he just wanted to let go. Young Dr. Pond was there, and Father Mike O'Brien too. After Joe died, everybody left the room, and I just sat with him for the longest time, holding his hand . . . ."

Only a handful of men now earn their living from herding sheep in the Taos Valley. Pacomio Mondragón is one of them, a cheerful, taciturn man from Llano Quemado who lives by the seasons, struggles hard to stay afloat, and is a staunch defender of the land. For years he was a major force in the Tres Rios Association during a struggle to keep a conservancy district and a Bureau of Reclamation dam from entering, and hastening the agricultural destruction of, the Taos Valley.

Two friends.

In the spring he drives his herd of ewes to a campsite on the Carson mesa a few miles southwest of Tres Orejas. One day I watched Pacomio and Andrés Martínez herd sheep across that mesa toward the Petaca Arroyo. The ewes knew exactly where to go, but sometimes the lambs strayed. When I was close to the herd, the noise was deafening; such unrelenting sheep babble, shrill baa-ing, frantic wailing. But when I retreated the cacophony almost subsided completely, swallowed up by the muffling omnipotence of rainy sky.

Andrés stooped over and shooed the animals ahead, guiding little lambs back into the flock. Sometimes he and Pacomio walked together, talking, almost oblivious to the sheep. But when animals strayed off, the two friends split apart, circled out, and chased the borregas back into the fold.

In this manner, they soon reached a trail descending into a gully that arrived at grassy banks near the bottom of the arroyo, a cleft miraculously full of water, a river almost half the width of the Rio Grande!

I was stunned. Normally, the Carson arroyos were empty. Usually, Pacomio had to ferry water in a tank truck over terrible roads from the Rio

Evening over Picuris Peak.

Grande to his campsite. But on this day, water draining from the porous reservoir after a heavy winter runoff was plentiful, and saved untold time and wear-and-tear on the vehicles.

From above, I watched the sheep cluster on the banks, drinking. Hummingbirds scissored noisily through the air. The entire scene had the quality of a mirage.

Seated on rocks, I overlooked that biblical illusion. Then I noticed at my feet, nestled on a slim ledge, four delicate mauve pasqueflowers . . . wild crocuses, I think they are also called.

A pure blossom in that dry territory—so delicate and out of place. When I looked up, most of the sheep were back on the trail, leaving the arroyo single-file, returning toward the camp.

In the distance shafts of sunlight that had broken through encircling webs of rain landed upon the sagebrush in theatrical colorful bursts, like fantasies of powdered gold.

FOUR

—

A Future

—

Up for

—

Grabs

—

Taos Ski Valley.

There is a profound and pervasive difference in the way Anglos and Spanish-Americans relate to land . . . Spanish-Americans tend to have an emotional attachment to the land (it is part of the family) and to value intimate, personal knowledge of one's own land and a continued lineal-family land ownership. They emphasize land transfer-and-use decisions based upon community welfare, along with the view that land ownership and usage established by custom are more important than those based upon legal documents. Anglos tend to view land as a commodity to be bought and sold if the price is right, and to stress maximum monetary income from land while they hold it.

> Clyde Eastman, Garrey Carruthers, and James A Liefer, "Contrasting Attitudes Toward Land in New Mexico"

Taos County may be beautiful, but it is not a happy environment for many of its nineteen thousand inhabitants. Only yesterday—May 6, 1977—the local social services director told me approximately 43 percent of the county is on one form of welfare or another. Although many long-

Ranchos de Taos Church.

term people (including those on welfare) tend to own their own houses, having kept them in the family, through inheritance, for centuries, much of that housing is now substandard: the subsistence infrastructure of mutual aid has broken down, and poor people have no cash for repairs. Within city limits outhouses are still common: over half the dwellings in the county lack adequate plumbing; a quarter of the houses are overcrowded. Outhouses, inadequate drainage in low-lying areas, poorly constructed septic tanks, and hand-dug wells mean that much of the water supply is polluted, leading to endemic low-profile diseases such as constant colds, which are a real drain on the poor. In town, there is very little low- or middle-income housing, especially for the elderly. And the wealthy in-migrants of recent years have driven real estate prices so high almost nobody local can afford to buy land or build decent houses.

Because at least half the population is extremely poor, the county has a weak tax base and cannot provide adequate services to meet growth needs. Already a new sewage plant, built to replace the old one which had been

High bridge over the gorge.

condemned by the EIA, is badly oversubscribed.

County unemployment is high. Official figures, almost always misleading, fail to include people not actively seeking employment. The work situation is so hopeless many jobless gave up long ago. Others pridefully reject the poverty occupations available here, choosing instead to eke out a living on their remaining tiny land parcels. Hence, although the official unemployment rate for Taos, according to Employment Security Commission statistics of two years ago, fluctuated from a high of 17.7 percent in February to a low of 10.4 in September, the actual rate is much higher. Immediately to the east and west, in largely Spanish-speaking Rio Arriba and Mora counties, the official unemployment rates for the same period were staggering: a high of 37.4 percent in Mora, 25.4 percent in Rio Arriba.

Most of the jobs available in this land of tourism and little else are service-oriented, low-paying, seasonal. They perpetuate poverty instead of alleviating it. Too, approximately ten thousand people in the Taos-Rio Arriba area work as migrant farmers in surrounding states during the growing season or for

Taos at twilight.

sheep outfits up North. U.S. Civil Rights Commission reports have said that many of these people are sometimes forced to work under conditions "resembling involuntary servitude or peonage."

In a recent survey I made, I found that of 132 businesses located at the heart of Taos, on or immediately around the Plaza, 107 (or approximately 80 percent) were owned by Anglos. In a town apocryphally rumored to be the world's third-largest art center (after Paris and New York) in terms of volume of paintings sold, 32 out of 36 galleries listed in the local phone book are Anglo-owned. Out of 23 listed real estate businesses, 21 are Anglo operations, as are two out of three major auto dealerships. Forty out of 52 listed restaurants are owned by more recent arrivals to the area, as are 10 out of the 12 listed sporting-goods operations. Fifty-four out of 57 listed motel and hotels are Anglo-owned. Ditto with both the local AM and FM radio stations. Listed Anglo contractors outnumber local contractors 15-3. Among professionals, such as lawyers, doctors, and dentists, the breakdown is equally lopsided: Anglo lawyers outnumber Chicano lawyers 19-4, Anglos

Clouds over Tres Orejas.

outnumber local doctors 19-2, and local dentists 7-1.

There is no question that long-term local Taoseños control the electoral politics, but the real economic power that guides society resides in relative newcomers' hands.

Over the last ten years, an influx of newcomers has enormously altered the area. Escapees from urban blight, often independently wealthy or folks who made a bundle in New York or Los Angeles, or people like myself who can earn a living outside the county, they have turned Taos upside down. And the Taos Valley is being changed from a stable, agrarian, Spanish-speaking area of strong individual communities held together by cultural ties, into a retirement, recreation, middle-class suburban, ghettoized urban mess, and the change is occurring with stunning rapidity. Little planning, lackluster zoning, and no overall philosophy are guiding it. The progress motto seems to be "every man for himself, and the devil take the hindmost."

Three Saturdays ago I was cleaning the Pacheco ditch beside an old man who told me: "I think we are almost at the end of this acequia farming. I

Old car, neighbor's yard.

think the ditch systems will collapse; I think it's almost over. All the local people are so discouraged. You can't earn a living off the land any more, or find fields to rent for your cattle."

J oe Mondragón was thirty-six years old and for a long time he had held no steady job. He had a wife, Nancy, and three children, and his own house, which he had built with his own hands, a small tight adobe that required mudding every two or three autumns.

Joe was always hard up, always hustling to make a buck. Over the years he had learned how to do almost any job. He knew everything about building houses, he knew how to mix mud and straw just right to make strong adobes that would not crumble. Though unlicensed, he could steal and lay his own plumbing, do all the electrical fixtures in a house, and hire five peons at slave wages to install a septic tank that would not overflow until the day after Joe died or left town. Given half the necessary equipment, he could dig a well, and he understood everything there was to understand about pumps. He could

Storm over Upper Ranchitos.

tear down a useless tractor and piece it together again so niftily it would plow like balls of fire for at least a week before blowing up and maiming the driver, and he could disk and seed a field well and irrigate it properly. "Hell," Joe liked to brag, "I could grow sweet corn just by using my own spit and a little ant piss!"

Joe had his own workshop crammed full of tools he had begged, borrowed, stolen or bought from various friends, enemies, and employers down through the years. In that shop he sometimes made skinning knives out of cracked buzz saw blades and sold them to hunters in the fall for five or six bucks. At the drop of a five-dollar bill he could also fashion an ornate Persian wine goblet from an old quart pop bottle. . . .

The Mondragón house was surrounded by junk, by old engines, by parts of motors, by automobile guts, refrigerator wiring, tractor innards. One shed was filled with wringer washer machines, and when Joe had the time he puttered over them until they were "running" again; then he tried—and often managed—to sell them . . . with pumps that went on the fritz (or wringer

Ten below zero, and far from home.

gears that neatly stripped themselves) ten minutes after Joe's three-month warranty (in writing) expired. This presented no problem, however, because for a very small consideration Joe was more than willing to fix whatever broke in whatever he had sold you.

But he was tired, Joe had to admit that. He was tired, like most of his neighbors were tired, from trying to earn a living off the land in a country where the government systematically gathered up the souls of little ranchers and used them to light its cigars. Joe was tired of spending twenty-eight hours a day like a chicken-thieving mongrel backed up against the barn wall, neck hairs bristling, teeth bared, knowing that in the end he was probably going to get his head blown off anyway. He was tired of meeting each spring with the prospect of having to become a migrant and head north to the lettuce and potato fields in Colorado where a man groveled under the blazing sun ten hours a day for one fucking dollar an hour. He was tired, too, of each year somehow losing a few cows off the permits he had to graze them on the government's National Forest land, and he was tired of the way permit

122

Winter in the valley.

fees were always being hiked, driving himself and his kind not only batty, but also out of business. And he was damn fed up with having to buy a license to hunt deer on land that had belonged to Grandfather Mondragón and his cronies, but which now resided in the hip pockets of either Smokey the Bear, the state, or the local malevolent despot, Ladd Devine the Third.

Usually, in fact, Joe did not buy a license to hunt deer in the mountains surrounding his hometown. Along with most everybody else in Milagro, he figured the dates of a hunting season were so much bullshit. If he hankered for meat, Joe simply greased up his .30-06, hopped into the pickup, and went looking for it. Once a Forest Service vendido, Carl Abeyta, had caught Joe with a dead deer, a huge electric lamp, no license, and out of season to boot, and it cost Joe a hundred dollars plus a week in the Chamisa County Jail. In jail he half-starved to death and was pistol-whipped almost unconscious by a county jailer, Todd McNunn, for trying to escape by battering a hole in the cheap cinderblock wall with his head.

Luke Nichols with a magic gorge ice wafer.

But Joe was tired of the fighting. Tired of it because in the end he never surfaced holding anything more potent than a pair of treys. In the end he just had his ass kicked from the corral to next Sunday, and nothing ever changed. In the end half his gardens and half his fields shriveled in a drought, even though Indian Creek practically formed a swimming pool in his living room. In fact, Milagro itself was half a ghost town, and all the old west side beanfields were barren, because over thirty-five years ago, during some complicated legal and political maneuverings known as the 1935 Interstate Water Compact, much of Milagro's Indian Creek water had been reallocated to big-time farmers down in the southeast portion of the state or in Texas, leaving folks like Joe Mondragón high and much too dry.

Los Córdovas is a small, largely agricultural settlement five miles southwest of Taos. Near the heart of the still-intact old plaza is a community center. Toward it, on a bright, sunny afternoon, I steer my truck, bouncing uncomfortably over the potholed dirt road. Beside me is Dr. Paul Sears, a

Paul Valerio, Andrés Martínez, Bernabé Chávez—leaders of the Tres Rios Association.

noted author, professor, and conservationist who must be in his nineties. Between his legs he holds a cane; on his lap rests a dated cross-section of a sagebrush trunk.

In the community center parking lot eight men are waiting. I help Dr. Sears out and shake hands with the men. Most are cattle or sheep ranchers who graze their animals on the mesa. After amenities, we all enter the building and get down to business.

Andrés Martínez chairs the gathering. These men . . . are concerned about their future on the mesa. Most have some reservations about how the Forest Service and BLM govern their lives west of the gorge. About wild river sections or transmission lines, they know little. What they do understand is that each year it's more difficult for them to eke out a living in that arid country.

No high passions or noisy rantings disrupt the meeting. These patient men keep their anger and frustrations under control. Yet the calm concern in their voices is sad to hear. Everybody remembers a time when things were

Flowering rabbitbrush.

better. Especially over fifty years ago when the mesa was a vast grassland the old-timers love to recall. Their memories are not in default: according to Dr. Sears, his dated sagebrush trunk proves that the plateau was once rich in forage grasses.

"We had thousands of animals living on that grass," one old man says quietly. "Then came the Floresta and the BLM. They said the land was overgrazed; they made us get off. That's when the sagebrush took over, when they started to 'manage' the land."

Another man backs him up. "It's like they do with the forest. I remember when the first planes came and sprayed the trees with insecticide near my ranch. My cows got sick. In one year I lost eleven head. When I opened them up their blood was clotted, like plasma; it was just like glue. But those insecticides didn't do any good. Look at the forest today—from Mora to Santa Fe the trees are dying of budworm. They control the forest so much, they stop all the fires, they eliminate most of the grazing until—heck—they manage the health right out of the forest. Today the forest is so inbred that the trees

126

More rain for the stock pond.

and all the animals have lost their hardiness. They have become diseased and weak and sickly."

Another problem they discuss involves Floresta policies requiring sheep permitees to move their camps every few days, even in mid-winter when snow covers the ground and little grazing damage can occur.

"Each time I have to move my camp it hurts my animals," says a plump rancher. "They get warm in one place, then have to move and bed down in cold snow. I'm not allowed to build a corral to protect the sheep. I'm trucking in hay, but they have to move anyway. I could plow off snow in each new area, but the Floresta won't let me bring in a tractor. They say they're trying to protect the mesa. But what about protecting *me?*"

"El dinero habla," laughs one old geezer. "Money talks."

For two hours the dialogue continues. I watch the faces. Chastisement of the government is meted out with irony and a sense of humor. At heart, most of the men are fatalistic. None carry an illusion that their way of life

Corner post on the mesa.

will survive much beyond themselves. When they die, most likely it will be over.

Several of the men are twice my age: I have known them for fifteen years. I hate to consider a Taos Valley (or my own life) without them. I think they stand for a strong history, a viable culture, and a healthy balance we can ill afford to lose around here (around anywhere).

And if their perceptions of life are reduced to quaint myth and nostalgic memory, this valley may succumb at last to the kind of cynical rootlessness that defines and cripples so much of America.

Meeting over, we saunter outside and mill around under a cloudless sky. The sun brilliantly bakes the parking lot. We all tarry, leaning against fenders, laughing, liking each other, making small talk. Sunshine permeates right to the bone; within moments we are laved in golden glow. Glancing around, I notice how much everyone appreciates the warmth, especially our oldest fogies, who keep talking, reluctant to leave, tenaciously hanging on to the moment.

River grasses.

"You know something?" says one of the octogenarians, "I just can't get enough of this damn sunshine. When I die, I wish they could fill up my grave with sunshine."

Without a doubt, the immediate future of this area is up for grabs. Despite the richness of cultures, the chaos here often defies imagination. Sometimes it seems as if Taos is caught in a riptide and is being helplessly dragged out to sea far beyond the reach of helping hands or benevolent philosophies. Although the population seems to remain fairly static at about nineteen thousand people, in the past eight years I have watched a phenomenal amount of building take place. The construction, the new developments, the commercial aspirations of the valley reflect the relentless in-migration of middle-class people, who are rapidly displacing the subsistence poor. Local cultures suffer because of this influx, and the land is taking it on the chin, from fragile irrigated valley pastures to the slopes of Wheeler Peak.

Lichen rock.

Permits are needed now to enter designated wild areas, and the wilderness designation itself often seems like a joke. On trails leading to Williams Lake, just below Wheeler Peak, the average backpacker is lucky not to be caught in a traffic jam: and the chipmunks are so civilized they are liable to mug him or her for their candy bars. I have stood on twelve-thousand-foot-high ridges in the Sangre de Cristos unable to see forty miles southward because of smog drifting up from Albuquerque, east from the Four Corners power plants, and in from the Taos Valley directly below. I have hiked into the beautiful Latir Lakes an hour north of Taos, and found them surrounded by garbage dumps, a hundred Boy Scouts slaughtering trout, or noisy out-of-staters guzzling beer. Snowmobiles and motorcycles unleash a constantly irritating engine noise high in the hills, and their trails are everywhere. Exploratory mineral cuts scar the mountains around Questa, and a poisonous dust from the moly mine's tailings lake often blows over that picturesque town. Several times, when I have been fishing the Red River below the mine, the water has suddenly become colored opaque lead from a line break above.

Crawdad skeleton.

To aid public relations, the mine is constantly stocking the river with fish, even as it petitions the government for permission to dump its wastes into the wild river section of the Rio Grande.

Citizens of Red River wish to build a transmountain road to the Taos Ski Valley, linking the two vacation resorts. Taos Ski Valley developers want to double the size of their village, placing a new town at the source of a river, the Hondo, which would further threaten the water supply feeding several downstream farming communities: Valdez, Des Montes, and Arroyo Hondo. Already that stream, lined as it is with camping areas, and polluted by sewage that often bypasses inadequate vacation-home systems, is one of the more polluted rivers in the state.

The county has, in the past, been decimated by carelessly constructed logging roads and by badly managed timber cutting. Erosion is a problem. Bald, formerly forested land at high elevations means that the snowmelt now occurs earlier and faster than in former times, contributing to erosion and making for irrigating crises during the summer. In Taos Canyon's Valle

Tiny paintbrush.

Escondido, dozens of tiny trout ponds built for summer tourists sap the Rio Fernando during the dry season, creating irrigation problems down below in the Cañon section of Taos. As irrigated valley land is taken from agricultural production for housing developments and shopping centers, as it is paved over or bisected by new roads, the water table sinks at an alarming rate, and private wells must be drilled ever deeper. New businesses like the Holiday Inn, with their hundreds of toilets, place further drain on limited water supply, making the lack of water a major crisis. At the same time the Forest Service hurts small ranchers by reducing grazing in order to maintain a "healthy forest," it promotes commercial enterprises such as mining and timbering, which put enormous pressures on our resources. In particular, the Floresta promotes tourism—that is, the influx of money-toting, and often super-destructive, people—an industry that compromises the natural environment as no cow or sheep ever could.

As in any impoverished area, alcoholism is rampant. Smack and cocaine are problems in and out of the schools, not to mention pot, liquor, and a

Miniature flower.

thousand variations on the upper-downer syndrome. Grotesque car accidents, usually involving strung-out teenagers, are much too frequent: the death toll in Taos County is abnormally high. Other kinds of violence, exacerbated by racial tensions, occasionally flare up. Everybody has a gun, and the weapons are often used. A friend of mine once raced around the Plaza busting plate-glass windows to draw the cops because some kids were trying to beat him up and rape his girlfriend. Seeking revenge, he drove out to where his tormentors lived, and shotgunned their automobiles. At Friday-night boogies, beatings and an occasional parking-lot rape have occurred often enough to be called almost common.

I lock my car as carefully here as I would in New York City; still, it has been ripped off three times. A good friend lost all his tools in broad daylight when he left his truck parked for five minutes before a restaurant. While an artist friend was out sketching primitive countryside, all four tires were stolen off her parked car. Burglaries are endemic: sometimes rifling houses seems to be the biggest industry in town. Fluorescent red signs

133

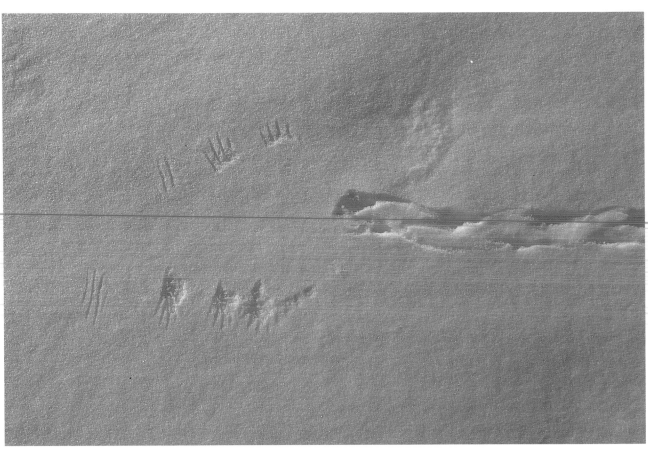

A horned lark took flight.

proclaiming NO TRESPASSING, PRIVATE PROPERTY, BEWARE OF DOG have proliferated as class gaps widen, the middle class becomes more predominant, and paranoia flourishes. A neighbor recently complained: "In the old days, when you killed a pig, all the neighbors would come around and help and you gave them some of the meat. Nowadays, when people are slaughtering an animal, they do it in private, they don't want anybody else to know, they don't want to share."

FIVE

—

We Shall

—

Advance

—

Together

—

Sunset, Taos foothills.

A danger of a book like this is that it will attract more people to the Taos area, thus accelerating the despoliation of a fragile valley. I have thought hard about this possibility. In the end, I concluded it would do no good to keep my mouth shut. People will move here no matter what. By the time I arrived in 1969, the rush was already on. All New Mexico lay on the block, as all of America has been on the block since the first Spaniards and the first Pilgrims came ashore bent on plunder. Taos history is no isolated story: what has happened and is happening here, went on and is going on across the nation.

Still, the change in twelve years has been real sobering. A majority of recent immigrants have only their self-interest at heart: it is the nature of our system to train people in this selfishness. Most territories are places to be exploited rather than cherished. Of course, some newcomers arrive with altruistic motives, like many Americans in Vietnam—and then they leave a shambles behind when they take a powder.

Dawn, Taos foothills.

The shambles occurs when land and people are treated solely as commodities.

In the long run, I feel it will do more good than harm for me to plead the case of this valley. Longtime locals here are not fragile, but many of them are tired. The toughest of them cannot be defeated, but they are mortal, and will die off. When that happens I see the valley becoming monolingual and monocultural, homogenized into a McDonald's and Sonic Burger mindset.

Toward the end of his book *Disturbing the Universe,* the nuclear physicist Freeman Dyson has a chapter entitled "Clades and Clones." *Clade,* he writes, is "a Greek word meaning a branch of a tree, in this case the evolutionary tree on which the twigs are individual species. When some climactic or geographical revolution occurs, upsetting the established balance of nature, not just one new species but a whole clade will appear within a geologically short time."

He next explains that the major evolutionary changes on earth have been caused by "the formation of new clades, rather than by the modification of

Rainbow over Talpa.

established species." This phenomenon occurs with cultural and social changes as well as within strictly biological evolutions. It accounts for the often frustrating, but incredibly rich and vital linguistic and cultural diversification on the globe.

A *clone,* Dyson then asserts, is the opposite of a clade. It is "a single population in which all individuals are genetically identical." In short, the makings of endless repetition.

"Clades are the stuff of which great leaps forward in evolution are made. Clones are evolutionary dead ends, slow to adapt, and slow to evolve. Clades can occur only in organisms that reproduce sexually. Clones in nature are typically asexual.

"All this," according to Dyson, "has its analog in the domain of linguistics. A linguistic clone is a monoglot culture, a population with a single language sheltered from alien words and alien thoughts." And, "in human cultures, as in biology, a clone is a dead end, a clade is a promise of immortality."

Finally, he asks the question, "Are we to be a clade or a clone? This is

141

Quiet time in February.

perhaps the central problem in humanity's future."

It is certainly a central problem in the future of Taos. This was once a highly original valley, with dark and mysterious sides, with lullabies and murderous intentions, with a profound veneration for the disturbing vitality of nature and human beings.

Currently, the drive is to vapidify all these qualities, making Taos a clone of the rest of the United States, ending forever its originality and polyglot cultures, cutting those mesas and mountains down to size with Bellamah-type homes and Kawasaki dirt bikes.

For the record, I doubt Taos or the rest of America can be saved short of a radical social and environmental revolution. I dread a violent conflagration within our borders. I pray that the simple state of the planet's resources may force even the passionate capitalists of our time to give up on planned obsolescence, and on the worship of an expand-or-expire syndrome.

If, somehow, we retain enough of the clade in our energetic society, we may adapt instead of creating a useless holocaust to prolong our conspicuous

consumption a few more years before all the oil runs out.

In the battle to change the destructive nature of our society, hope for the future is a potent weapon against the manipulative cynicism of the *sauve-qui-peut,* every-person-for-themselves mentality of our economic system, which depends on an alienated and ruthlessly competitive populace for its survival.

I insist on a hopeful outlook. I trust I will always have the courage to insist on this attitude, no matter how desperate the situation appears to be. This does not mean that I am a hopeless idealist, or an innocent romantic. It means simply that in order to work for the salvation of the planet, we *must* believe in its future. We must love life, love America, love the Taos Valley.

I think profit motives derive their strength from despair. If we accept the end of the world, what's to stop us from hastening the inevitable while making hay while the sun shines? I see capitalism founded on this principle: socialism makes a lot more human and ecological sense to me . . . although

Moon over frozen stock pond.

everyone is going to have to redefine the nature of materialism in the next fifty years, Communists included.

Pablo Neruda has said it for me:

I still have absolute faith in human destiny, a clearer and clearer conviction that we are approaching a great common tenderness. I write knowing that the danger of the bomb hangs over all our heads, a nuclear catastrophe that would leave no one, nothing on this earth. Well, that does not alter my hope. At this critical moment, in this flicker of anguish, we know that the true light will enter those eyes that are vigilant. We shall all understand one another. We shall advance together. And this hope cannot be crushed.

Momentary despair does not make me panic. Only an icy soul would not often despair over the cruel machinations that systematically massacre great sectors of humankind. Nevertheless, it is important not to wallow in the tragedies of Auschwitz and Vietnam. Those dark forces are constantly afoot,

Sunset, Tres Orejas.

concocting plagues that riddle the human spirit—granted. Yet they are not all-powerful; Life . . . all the great tintinabulations of the senses . . . plus the mighty adventures within the struggle each day to shape a new blossom . . . forbids it.

Therefore, I am certain nobody is going to protect the dynamic and positive roots of Taos by hiding the fact that this area exists. That would leave it defenseless against the outer world. It must be very clear to all of us who feel a stake in the future of Taos and our country, and thus in the world, that, as Joseph Conrad once made indisputably clear in his novel *Victory,* the outer world always arrives.

Frankly, I don't think you can emphasize enough the beauty of what should be preserved for future generations. Too often we negate the simple things that once nourished our lives: repeatedly, our forgetful memories need jogging.

What I have to say about Taos pertains to everywhere. Taos is only a metaphor for that entire continent F. Scott Fitzgerald once imagined as the

145

Huerfano Mountain, on the mesa.

last piece of terrain wild and beautiful enough to be commensurate with our capacity for wonder. Hence, my defense of this small territory should speak to all of us, from the Arctic Circle to the lattermost mist-shrouded island south of Tierra del Fuego.

Often Spanish-speaking people approach me, asking, "How could you know so much about our culture—after living in Taos for only two and a half years—to write your novel, *The Milagro Beanfield War?*"

My response is that ninety percent of the novel is universal. Similar struggles, cultures, and people exist in such disparate places as New York City, rural Vermont, Virginia, France, Spain, and Guatemala.

This understanding was a part of my sensibility long before I arrived in New Mexico.